A WITCH'S GUIDE TO GHOSTS AND THE SUPERNATURAL

By
Gerina Dunwich

NEW PAGE BOOKS
A division of The Career Press, Inc.
Franklin Lakes, NJ

A WITCH'S GUIDE TO GHOSTS AND THE SUPERNATURAL
EDITED AND TYPESET BY NICOLE DEFELICE
Cover design by Lu Rossman/Digi Dog Design
Printed in the U.S.A. by Book-mart Press

To order this title, please call toll-free 1-800-CAREER-1 (NJ and Canada: 201-848-0310) to order using VISA or MasterCard, or for further information on books from Career Press.

The Career Press, Inc., 3 Tice Road, PO Box 687,
Franklin Lakes, NJ 07417
www.careerpress.com
www.newpagebooks.com

Library of Congress Cataloging-in-Publication Data

Dunwich, Gerina.
    A witch's guide to ghosts and the supernatural / by Gerina Dunwich.
        p. cm.
    Includes bibliographical references and index.
    ISBN 1-56414-616-2 (pbk.)
        1. Ghosts. 2. Witchcraft. 3. Magic. 4. Charms I. Title.

BF1471 .D86 2002
133--dc21

2002066036

Also by Gerina Dunwich:

Dedication/ Acknowledgments

With love and gratitude do I dedicate this book to my mother, who told me my first ghost story when I was a child; to Al for assisting me with research for this book; and to my cousin Dave, who was by my side when I cast my first spell and attended my first séance.

I also wish to thank everyone who helped to make this book possible, especially Stephany (for being the best agent in the world); Nicole DeFelice, my editor at New Page Books; Tamara Thorne; Sirona Knight; Karri Ann Allrich; Lee Prosser; Jeffrey Parish; and Tim Braun.

Contents

Foreword

"Whether ill-behaved or benevolent, spiritual or quasi-material, bedmates or strangers, ghosts are universal; they haunt virtually every culture, Eastern and Western."
—Jack Sullivan, *The Penguin Encyclopedia of Horror and the Supernatural*

Ghosts and the supernatural have been a part of my existence for as long as I can remember. My attraction to ghosts developed early in life and a psychic once told me that I was born with something unusual in my aura that attracted ghosts to me. Undoubtedly, some people—especially those of the ghost-dreading variety—may perceive this as a kind of curse. However, I have always considered it to be a gift from the gods. As a child, I was intensely drawn to the world of the occult and fascinated greatly by ghost stories (especially those belonging to the category of non-fiction), haunted dwellings, communication with the dead, and the ancient legends of vampires and werewolves.

I attended my first séance in the late sixties with my cousins Carol and David, along with a couple of teenage girls who lived in the neighborhood. It was held on the pillared half-moon porch of my Grandmother Rose's old house in Riverside, Illinois, and the spirit we summoned that summer night was none other than that of the assassinated president, Abraham Lincoln. I can still recall the rush of adrenaline that surged through my body as I, along with everyone else who had attended the séance, witnessed the figure of a tall man in black suddenly appear in the middle of the street and begin walking past the house. Oddly, he would take a few paces, vanish, and then reappear about nine or 10 feet ahead of where he had been. He continued to walk, vanish, and then reappear in this strange manner until he reached the end of the street and was no longer in our view.

I also knew intuitively at a very young age that my grandmother's house was inhabited by the spirit of my late grandfather, who had succumbed to cancer many years before I was born. Without knowing why, I had always feared being alone in a certain bedroom located at the top of the stairs to the left. I felt it had the strangest energy about it, and it always gave me the uneasy feeling that someone was in there watching me even though there would be nobody in the room with me. I was not aware until many years later that the empty room that had frightened me as a child was, in fact, the very room in which my grandfather had died while in his bed.

My interest in, and encounters with, ghosts and the supernatural continued into my adulthood. During my travels, I once spent a night in a haunted hotel room outside of

Buffalo, New York, where the dresser drawers and closet door kept opening by themselves. Each time I closed them and returned to bed, I woke up later to find them all open again. On a Halloween night more than a decade later, I was watching an interesting television program about various haunted hotels throughout the United States and discovered then that the hotel where I had stayed near Buffalo had a local reputation for being haunted. The televised documentary went on to mention that in one of the hotel's bedrooms, where a guest had either died or been murdered (I can't recall which), numerous witnesses reported seeing the closet door and drawers of the dresser opening by themselves at night!

During another one of my trips to the East Coast, I slept overnight in an historic century-old hotel in Portland, Maine. Shortly after midnight, I was roused from my sleep by the faint tinkling sound of tiny bells being rung. The following morning I discovered two small and very old copper bells sitting on the table next to the bed. (The bells had not been there when I went to bed the night before.) After examining them closely and finding numbers etched inside, I wrapped the bells in a tissue and put them in my purse. However, when I went to retrieve them a few hours later to show them to someone, I found they had mysteriously vanished.

In the spring of 1984, shortly after moving to the New England community of Beverly, Massachusetts (on the North Shore of Boston), my significant other and I headed to the nearby historic city of Salem to check out some of the local attractions. Among them, an overpriced occult shop tended by two rather unsociable young ladies, and the Salem Witch Dungeon Museum, which, in my humble opinion, no person visiting Salem, Massachusetts, should leave out of their itinerary! For Al and I, however, the highlight of that day's excursion was undoubtedly the guided tour we took of the House of Seven Gables.

Built in the year 1668 (24 years prior to the infamous witchcraft trials and hangings that were held in Salem Village in the year 1692), the House of Seven Gables is said to be the oldest wooden mansion still standing in all of New England. It is also the house that inspired author Nathaniel Hawthorne to write his legendary novel, which bore the same name.

Upon setting foot in the house to take the tour, I couldn't help but feel overwhelmed by a strange and intense paranormal vibration that I can only describe, for lack of a better term, as "ghost energy." As the tour guide led us from room to room and even up a narrow secret staircase, I noticed that this ghost energy seemed to fluctuate, being stronger in some parts of the house and not as strong in others, yet always present. But it was in the attic where I felt it to be the most intense. I looked around at the others in the tour group and wondered to myself if any of them could feel it as well. However, judging by their facial expressions and body language, they all appeared to be quite oblivious to it.

After entertaining the group with a few interesting anecdotes, such as how cows' milk was used in the making of paint in the 17th Century, our guide led us from the attic into another part of the house. But I had the overwhelming urge to return there. When no one was looking, Al and I wandered away from the group and sneaked back into the attic for another look. Not more than 10 or 15 seconds had passed before we both witnessed a small empty wooden rocking chair in the far corner begin to rock back and forth at a fast pace as though someone were sitting in it. We could hardly believe what our eyes were seeing and I suddenly began to feel extremely light-headed, not realizing at that moment that something in the room was trying to feed off of my energy. While I stood in the doorway keeping watch, Al went over to the rocker and carefully examined it to see if it had been rigged with any wires or strings. There were none to be found. We rejoined the others in the group and said nothing of our bizarre experience to anyone. And, not surprisingly, the farther we got from the attic, the less light-headed I felt. When the tour of the historic mansion finally concluded, Al and I left knowing that our experience in the House of Seven Gables would be one we'd truly remember for the rest of our lives.

In January of the following year, Al and I moved into an apartment in Ipswich, Massachusetts, and lived there for six months before moving back to the West Coast. It was during that time that Al worked a part-time night job cleaning the inside of an old utility company. On more than one occasion, he reported to me about hearing strange sounds and feeling that he wasn't alone while working there and being alone in the building. Intrigued (as I usually am whenever it comes to the supernatural), I decided to accompany him to work one night.

We arrived there around 10 p.m. and, while Al was busy getting his janitorial supplies from a storage room in the back, I wandered about the building, eventually making my way up to the front office. As I opened the door, I was startled by the unexpected sight of an old man dressed from head to toe in black attire reminiscent of clothing styles from a past century. I asked what he was doing there and if he was an employee of the utility company. He gave me a rather strange smile, and an even stranger answer. He told me that he lived there.

Immediately thinking that this odd gentleman might have been a mentally disturbed, or perhaps an intoxicated individual who had managed to break into the building either to steal something or take refuge, I politely excused myself and then rushed to the other side of the building to alert Al. He and I returned to the front office but found no one there. Then we heard from down the hall the sound of the men's restroom door open and slam shut. Assuming the man I had seen and spoke to in the front office had gone into the restroom, Al knocked upon the door and asked him if he was all right in there, but got no reply. He then attempted to open the door but it felt to him as though someone was on the other side pushing against it and preventing him from opening it more than an inch or so. I was beginning to think that the old man had passed out in the restroom and his body was on the floor blocking the door.

After several attempts, Al was suddenly able to push the door open without the slightest effort, but when he and I entered the room, we were stunned to find nobody in there! With no window or other door leading out of that restroom, there was no possible way for that man to have gotten out, unless, of course, he simply vanished into thin air, which is typically the way ghosts make their departures.

This was not to be our last paranormal experience at the utility company. On another night, Al and I were suddenly showered with paper clips that materialized out of nowhere as we walked down the corridor, and there was also the time I happened upon a sheet of typing paper sticking out of a typewriter in one of the back rooms. Upon it had been typed some sort of strange verse that sounded like it could have been a passage from the Bible. I felt compelled to take the paper with its cryptic message home with me, so I plucked it from the typewriter, folded it twice, and then put it inside my purse for safekeeping. Later that evening when we arrived back at our apartment, I immediately retrieved the paper from my purse and unfolded it, only to find the words that had been typed so clearly upon it were no longer there!

While I will be the first to admit that some of my encounters with the supernatural may sound incredible, I can assure you, Witch's honor, that every one of them is completely true and recalled from my memory as accurately as possible. (However, to protect the privacy of others, I have deliberately left out complete street addresses and person's last names in many instances.)

My paranormal experiences have been many, and I have also had the great fortune to live in several haunted houses in various parts of the country. Among them, a 1950s ranch house in Southern California, a 300-year-old Colonial house in Massachusetts known as the Moses Day Homestead, and an old Victorian mansion in a small country town in upstate New York. My lifelong interest in, and experiences with, the spirits of the dead eventually led me to become involved in spirit channeling, ghost research, the investigation of haunted houses, and the writing of this book.

> "The supernatural is always with us. Even though we tend to laugh them off in this modern world, unexplained mysteries occur all the time."
> —Susy Smith, *A Supernatural Primer for the Millions*

Introduction

Ghosts and the supernatural have intrigued and terrified mankind since the dawn of history. Some people simply dismiss both as being nothing more than mere superstition or the products of an overactive imagination. However, anyone who has ever witnessed a ghostly manifestation or unexplained supernatural phenomena firsthand knows differently.

Ask just about anyone who disbelieves in the existence of ghosts and spirits if they have ever encountered one, and most likely their reply would be that they have not, nor would they ever expect to. This does not mean that only those who believe in them are privy to see them. While some people who have encountered a ghost or a spirit have always been open-minded to the existence of such things, many were indeed skeptical and disbelieving until their own encounters made believers out of them.

Skeptics may argue that ghosts exist only in people's minds, and while I will wholeheartedly agree that some ghostly manifestations are simply the result of overactive imaginations, I must emphatically state that this is not always the case! Sometimes the creaking of the stairs is not caused by the settling of the house, nor is the fleeting shadow on the wall a trick of the eye, nor the eerie moaning emanating from the darkness of the attic merely the wailing of the wind. Sometimes the so-called "things that go bump in the night" are, in fact, part of the intriguing and unexplained phenomena we know quite simply as ghosts and hauntings.

Spirits can appear to anyone at any time and in just about any place, scaring the wits out of those who never fathomed that such a thing could actually happen, and making bona fide believers out of many non-believers.

If the death of an individual was sudden and unexpected, it is not at all uncommon for their spirit to remain at or near the site where their death took place. They are often confused and unaware, or not willing to accept, the fact that they are no longer alive. They will typically attach themselves to the area and attempt to make contact with any and all spirit-sensitive persons who happen to pass by. These kinds of spirits are basically harmless and often in need of our help to enable them to find peace. They can be found in just about any location that has been the scene of a tragic death, including murders and accidents.

I know that ghosts and spirits are real because I have seen and communicated with a number of them since childhood, and I know many other people who have as well. Some of these people are friends and family members, and some are individuals whom I have met over the years during my travels. Every ghost and every haunting are different, yet all are bound by one common factor: They prove that death is not necessarily the final ending.

> "Public opinion polls indicate that approximately 25 percent of Americans believe that ghosts really can haunt a house, and roughly 67 percent believe in life after death."
> —Patricia D. Netzley, *Haunted Houses*

In *The Ghostly Register*, author Arthur Myers says, "Students of the spiritual take the view that when we die each of us drops our physical body but retains another body, similar but vibrating at different frequencies." Upon death, the natural course is to exit the physical plane and graduate to a higher spiritual realm. However, some spirits remain earthbound for many different reasons, such as love, greed, fear of moving on, attachment to a particular person or place, and so forth.

Where apparitions are concerned, there are basically two types that exist. The first is nothing more than an imprint of energy left behind in a place by a person who had once been alive there. The person is no longer there, but their image remains. According to Myers, "the energy carryover [as he refers to this type of apparition] goes strictly about its own business, oblivious of our time and space and probably of anything else." The second type of apparition (which Myers calls the "real ghosts") is the actual spirit of a person who remains attached to a certain place. Unlike the first type of apparition—the energy carryover— these apparitions are said to be aware of our physical plane and capable of interacting with the living. For clarification, some parapsychologists simply refer to the first type of apparition as "ghosts," and to the second as "spirits."

The typical Christian view of ghosts is that they are not spirits of the dead at all, but actually wicked demons dispatched by God's infernal adversary, Satan, to deceive and to harm. In an online article entitled, *Are Demons Real?* (Bible Theology Ministries, United Kingdom, June 1992) K.B. Napier claims, "*all* ghosts without exception, are demons." He also goes on to state that, "Ghosts are never friendly. They are always wicked, even if they appear to be kind."

Even many individuals who are not Christians tend to be of the mind that ghosts are evil, or are at least capable of bringing physical injury or death to the living if that happened to be their desire. My late father is an ideal example of a non-Christian's fear of ghosts. He was an atheist, yet he still believed in the existence of ghosts and even admitted once to his irrational fear of them.

I believe such fears can be attributed in part, or in whole, to mankind's innate fear of both death and the unknown—two of the realms to which all ghosts belong. Fictional novels and horror movies also add to this fear by projecting into our minds the images of ghosts as fearful evil entities bent on attacking and terrifying the living, sometimes motivated by revenge, but often for no apparent reason, as though it were simply the common nature of ghosts to be malevolent and malicious. But whatever the reasons, there are people from all walks of life who continue to be terrified of ghosts and see them as something potentially harmful.

Professor Hans Holzer, a renowned parapsychologist and prolific author, believes otherwise. In his book, *Ghosts: True Encounters with the World Beyond*, he states, "Ghosts have never harmed anyone except through fear found within the witness, of his own doing and because of his own ignorance as to what ghosts represent." Although he does acknowledge that there are a small number of cases of ghosts attacking the living, he believes them to be "simply a matter of mistaken identity, where extreme violence at the time of death has left a strong residue of memory in the individual ghost."

In *The Field Guide to Ghosts and Other Apparitions*, authors Hilary Evans and Patrick Huyghe raise an interesting question: "Why aren't ghosts naked?" Sightings of naked ghosts are rare, and most apparitions are reported seen wearing the same clothes they wore when alive. This would make one wonder, then, if clothing has ethereal counterparts, or if the clothing worn by a person's spirit is merely some sort of projected image he or she uses out of a sense of modesty, to keep from offending the living, or perhaps to be recognized? As it seems to always be the case, the minute we attempt to understand ghosts in human terms, we find ourselves confronted by absurdity.

Another valid question brought up by Evans and Huyghe is: "Do ghosts exist when nobody is looking at them?" Granted, this is purely a philosophical question to which it is impossible to give a definite answer. It falls along the same lines as the age-old question: "If a tree falls in the middle of a forest and nobody is there to hear it, does it still make a sound?" We naturally assume that it does, although we have no real way to be absolutely and unequivocally sure.

I am personally of the opinion that ghosts most definitely do exist even when there is nobody around. I base this not only on my own intuitive feelings, but on the fact that there have been a number of ghosts whose images have been caught on the tape of video cameras set up in rooms or other areas where no human was physically present at the time of the manifestations.

Chapter 1

Phantasms and Ectoplasms

"Millions of spiritual creatures walk the earth unseen, both when we wake, and when we sleep."
—John Milton, *Paradise Lost*

Understanding Ghosts and Spirits

Despite what some individuals may think, not all people who die automatically become a ghost, which explains why mediums and channelers are able to make contact with certain spirits and not others. I personally believe that, after a natural death, most people's spirits either find eternal peace by entering what is known as "the light," or they go on to reincarnate. However, the spirits of many who die tragic deaths—especially by murder or suicide, those who are unwilling to accept their death or unaware that they are in fact dead, and those who have important unfinished business in the physical plane or are strongly attached to a certain person, place, or inanimate object, remain earthbound until they are ready to move on. Spirits can sometimes remain earthbound for a short while, for centuries, or for all of eternity.

Depending upon the individual spirit, moving on can take place as soon as a certain mission is accomplished, once they realize they are dead, after being forgiven for something bad they may feel responsible for, or when a person with mediumistic abilities lovingly guides them into the light.

Some ghost researchers believe that fear is one of the main reasons that a spirit chooses to remain earthbound instead of crossing over. Fear of such things as the unknown, the termination of one's existence, judgment and punishment for past deeds, and Hell, can be strong enough to hold a spirit back from going into the light. Such spirits remain trapped between our dimension and the next simply out of their own fears.

Guilt is another common reason for spirits to remain behind. They may feel that by dying they have left their loved ones (especially children) alone, uncared for, or financially burdened. Those who commit suicide or die in some way by their own actions (such as an accidental drug overdose or losing at a deadly game of Russian Roulette) often experience great guilt in the afterlife for ending their lives or contributing to their own death, and, in some cases (such as fatal automobile crashes caused by drug or alcohol use or reckless driving), the deaths or serious injuries of others.

Sometimes one's love for, and inability or unwillingness to let go of, someone who has died can be powerful enough to keep his or her spirit earthbound. Only after the living's obsession with the deceased is overcome and they are finally able to come to terms with the loss of their loved one can the earthbound spirit feel it is able to cross over.

Ghosts vs. Spirits

According to the *Merriam-Webster's Collegiate Dictionary*, the definition of a ghost is "a disembodied soul; especially the soul of a dead person believed to be an inhabitant of the unseen world or to appear to the living in

bodily likeness." It comes from the Old English *gast*; akin to the Old High German *geist*, meaning, "spirit."

The word "spirit" is defined as "a supernatural being or essence; an often malevolent being that is bodiless but can become visible; a malevolent being that enters and possesses a human being." It comes from the Latin *spiritus*, which means "breath."

Most people throughout the world use the words "spirit" and "ghost" interchangeably. However, while both of these entities may be an apparition of a person no longer living, there exists a significant difference between the two.

Spirits, which are generally regarded as "non-haunting apparitions," appear to be aware of their surroundings and of the persons around them and observing them. On the other hand, ghosts, which are regarded as "haunting apparitions," seem to be completely unaware of their surroundings and of the presence of the living. And unlike spirits, which often manifest for a particular reason and might attempt to communicate with the living, a ghost typically haunts the same location (in most cases the scene of its death), repeating the same actions again and again, much like a series of images recorded on a videotape that are played back repeatedly. Additionally, very few people who encounter a ghost during one of its hauntings ever report that the apparition tries to establish communication with them.

Poltergeist Phenomena

The word *poltergeist* comes from the German *Polter*, "uproar," and *Geist*, "ghost." It is given to the type of ghostly phenomenon in which sudden disturbances, such as loud rapping and other sounds, the throwing of objects, the moving of furniture, strange lights, peculiar odors, and physical assaults upon humans and animals, occur.

Another common characteristic of a poltergeist experience is lithobolia. This is the phenomenon of pebbles or small stones materializing out of thin air and raining down upon a person, a house, or an area. In such cases, witnesses report seeing the objects falling from the sky (and even from ceilings) or being thrown by unseen hands, sometimes changing direction abruptly during their course of travel.

Poltergeist activity at times is also responsible for peculiar incidents involving water (such as the sudden and unexplained appearance of puddles on a floor, broken water pipes, faucets turning on and off by themselves, etc.) and spontaneous fires of undetermined origin.

"Poltergeists are spirits that seem intent on causing trouble."
—Patricia D. Netzley

There are a number of ways in which poltergeists differ from ordinary ghosts. The most apparent is their violent nature. Poltergeist activity frequently happens during daylight hours, whereas the majority of other haunting phenomena seem to take place at night. It can also begin quite suddenly, for no apparent reason, and end just as suddenly—after months or even years. And unlike most of your ordinary run-of-the-mill hauntings, poltergeist phenomena seldom involve apparitions. When one does manifest, it is usually difficult for witnesses or researchers to link it to a specific deceased person. Poltergeist activity can sometimes follow an individual from place to place, whereas a classic ghost haunting always repeats in the same location, often each time at the same hour of the day or night or at a particular time of the year, such as an anniversary date of a death.

Many believe that poltergeist activity can be attributed to one of two things: In other cases it is a mischievous or malevolent spirit possessing the ability to move objects by solidifying the ambient air, which results in the movement and teleportation of objects. Or, that it is not the work of spirits, but rather the subconscious psychokinetic powers of a pubescent child or an individual undergoing a great amount of stress.

Cold Spots and Spirit Portals

A sudden and unexplained drop in temperature that occurs in an area where poltergeist activity, a haunting, or a spirit visitation is taking place is known as a "cold spot." Certain psychic-sensitive individuals are often able to feel cold spots in cemeteries (particularly at gravesides), morgues, and other places where death is present.

In many haunted houses there is one room or area—often the site of a tragic death, murder, or suicide—where the temperature is lower, and electro-magnetic readings are higher, than in other parts of the dwelling. This is commonly referred to as "the heart of the house," and in many cases will prove to be the location of most or all of the phenomena, such as poltergeist activity and/or spirit manifestations, which occur within the place.

Some people believe that cold spots indicate the locations of spirit portals, or invisible doorways between our world and the spiritual dimension, through which the spirits can pass in and out. Many also believe that working with Ouija boards (or similar devices) or holding séances to contact spirits of the deceased can create, or unlock if you will, such a door through which the summoned spirit enters and leaves our plane of existence. Normally, after communication with the spirit is ended and the departing entity returns to its own world, the spirit portal closes behind it. However, in some instances the portal remains open. When this happens, there is typically an increase in ghost activity in the house or area. The only ways to close these spirit portals is through prayer or spell.

I once observed an acquaintance of mine—a modern day Druid—close a number of spirit portals by placing the palm of one of his hands against each cold spot and then slowly turning it counter-clockwise while visualizing it being sealed up. It was an interesting technique that I had never before seen applied, but it seemed to work rather effectively.

To Dream About a Ghost

Some folks are of the belief that ghosts seen in their dreams are actual representations of the dead. However, many dream interpreters feel that this is the most unlikely explanation for this type of dream, suggesting instead that the dream-ghost actually represents a part of the dreamer that is not clear or understood. It can also symbolize certain aspects of ourselves that we fear. This may involve a painful memory, feelings of guilt, or certain thoughts that have been repressed. Such a dream may also reveal a fear of death or dying. Alternatively, when ghosts materialize in our dreams they sometimes represent things that are elusive, out of reach, or no longer obtainable to us.

According to some psychologists, dreaming about the ghost of a dead friend or loved one may be an indication of guilt and regrets concerning the dreamer's past relationships with that particular individual.

Many old dream dictionaries that base their interpretations on folklore and superstition claim that dreaming of friendly ghosts portends unexpected good luck. However, dreaming about frightful ghosts supposedly denotes that others will attempt to impose their will upon you, and the only way to overcome them is to be vigilant.

Some people regard a dream in which a ghost simply appears as an omen of good luck, while dreams involving ghosts that speak to or frighten the dreamer are seen as a warning that the dreamer will be greatly pressured to take part in a scheme or activity that goes against his or her principles. (If this should be the case for you, resist the temptation with all the strength you can muster, and if necessary, turn to a trusted friend or adviser for help.)

To dream about a faceless ghost indicates that the source of something (depending upon the circumstances and other symbols of the dream) has not yet been identified. For instance, a faceless ghost that fills the dreamer with feelings of fear could mean that he or she needs to examine the cause of a phobia, or face one's fear, in order to overcome it.

To dream that you are making love with a ghostly stranger may indicate a relationship or affair without substance or a lover who is untrue. If a widow or widower has a romantic dream involving the ghost of their departed spouse, this indicates a love that survives the grave. However, it is said that when an elderly or gravely ill person begins to experience recurring dreams about a deceased spouse or other relatives who are dead, this is a sign that death is near.

While researching this section of the book, I consulted a number of dream interpretation books. In one of them, Gustavus Hindman Miller's *10,000 Dreams Interpreted*, I found the following interpretations for various types of dreams involving ghosts and spirits:

To dream about the ghost of your mother or father is said to denote the threat of danger. It may also be a warning to be cautious when forming new partnerships with people you do not know very well.

To dream about the ghost of a beloved friend is said to portend a long journey with an unpleasant companion. Be prepared to receive a number of disappointments.

If a man dreams that a ghost is speaking to him, this warns that he will be lured into the hands of his enemies. For a woman, such a dream is a grim omen of widowhood and deception.

To dream that a ghost appears in the sky is said to be an omen of misfortune or possibly the death of a loved one. If you dream that you see in the sky a male ghost on your right and a female ghost on your left, this indicates "a quick rise from obscurity to fame," according to Miller. However, your fame will prove to be short-lived "as death will be a visitor and will bear you off."

To dream about a female ghost in long robes floating peacefully in the air portends sudden wealth accompanied by sorrow. Miller says that such a dream may also indicate "progress in scientific studies."

To dream about the ghost of a person who is still alive is said to be a warning that the dreamer is in danger from a spiteful friend or acquaintance. It may also indicate the ending of a friendship. If the person's ghost appears lean and gaunt, such a dream may portend the early death of that individual.

To dream that a ghost is pursuing you warns of unusual and disquieting experiences in the near future. However, if you dream that the ghost is fleeing from you, this is a sure sign that your coming troubles will be to a lesser degree and/or overcome quickly.

Unexpected trouble will come to call if you dream about spirits or specters, according to Miller. If they are seen wearing robes of white, this is an omen that a close friend will soon take ill. If they are draped in robes of black, be prepared for treachery and unfaithfulness. It is also said that unexpected troubles will soon arise for those who dream about spirits rapping upon doors or walls.

Dreaming that spirits are hiding or moving behind draperies warns against committing indiscretions.

To dream that you hear spirits singing forlornly or playing music indicates that your household will soon meet with unfavorable changes and sadness. To dream that a spirit is ringing a bell is a grave omen, foretelling the death of a friend or relative.

According to Nerys Dee's *The Dreamer's Workbook*, to dream that a ghost is standing by your bedside indicates a visitation from the spirit world. Dee also says that dreams involving ghosts reflect "the spiritual nature of the dreamer." When a spirit appears in a dream, it may either represent a past memory or the ghost of a deceased person.

Dreams that involve haunted houses usually signify repressed memories and feelings that need to be acknowledged. They may also reveal that there exists unfinished emotional business relating to the dreamer's childhood and/ or family.

To dream that a ghost is haunting you in some way clearly indicates that you are feeling haunted by something or someone from your past.

To dream about a walking ghost is said to be an omen that financial difficulties will soon plague you. Take care not to spend your money foolishly or allow yourself to become deeper in debt.

A dream in which a ghost in white appears has long been regarded as a sign of good luck, while one in which a ghost in black is seen indicates illness or bitterness between the dreamer and his or her lover.

A dream in which you see yourself as a ghost may be trying to tell you in a symbolic way that you are living in the past too much or are feeling that a part of you (figuratively speaking) is dead. For a writer or an artist to experience such a dream may very well indicate the opportunity to do literary or artistic work for another (as in being a "ghost-writer").

To dream that others perceive you as a ghost may mean that you are deeply worried that people might look at you as someone with an outmoded way of thinking or doing things.

To dream that you are trying to conjure up or contact a ghost without success may be a symbolic message from your inner self to "give up the ghost" where something futile is concerned. Through another play on words (which dreams oftentimes are), this dream may be indicating that you haven't "the ghost of a chance."

Communicating With Spirits Through Dreams

There are a wide variety of ways in which the spirits of the dead are able to communicate with the living—séances, Ouija boards, and necromantic rites are several examples, which are covered in detail in other chapters of this book.

On those occasions when we experience the eerie feeling of not being alone or of being watched when no one else is around, there is a good chance that a spirit is close at hand and may be attempting to communicate with us or, in the very least, make its presence known. Some spirits prefer to write their messages, while others whisper them in the wind. Some have even been known to use the telephone to make their contact with the living—a phenomenon unquestionably dramatic, but hardly uncommon.

The giving of signs—whether they are cryptic or evident—is another one of the ways in which spirits transmit their messages. And dreams are yet another, and perhaps the most common, way for the dead to contact us. It is believed that many spirits choose the avenue of dream communication because it is considerably less frightening to the living to receive a visitation from a spirit while in the dream state, as opposed to while in the waking state. Also, when we are sleeping, our minds are open to many things that we may not be receptive to while in the waking state.

Nearly everyone has at least once in his or her lifetime experienced a dream involving someone who was deceased. However, not all such dreams are actual encounters with spirits on the astral plane. Many are merely dreams and nothing more. Sometimes it can be difficult to distinguish between the two.

Typically a dream that is an actual spirit encounter will involve a beloved friend, a relative, or someone who the dreamer was close to. The spirit of such an individual may be perceived in the dream as either being a ghost or a living person, and will often have a message of some sort to pass along to the dreamer. This can be anything from a simple expression of their love, to a confession of a past deed, to the revelation of a secret. In some instances, spirit messages that come through in dreams are prophetic in nature, and become validated at the time when such prophecies are fulfilled.

Dreams of this nature normally feel more "real" than one's regular dreams, and are more vivid and intense as well. It is not uncommon for lucid dreams (dreams in which the dreamer is aware that he or she is in a dream state) to host spirit visitations.

Sometimes when an individual is headed for great danger, the apparition of a deceased family member—in many cases a parent or grandparent—will appear in one of that individual's dreams with words of warning. The spirits of loved ones have also been known to appear in the dreams of persons who are close to death. In these cases, the spirit's mission is usually to comfort the dreamer by alleviating fears of death, letting it be known that loved ones are waiting on the other side, and gently preparing the individual for his or her inevitable crossing over into death.

Just as the dead can utilize the dreams of the living to communicate from beyond the grave, so too can the living make use of their dreams to make contact with those who have died. In order to do this, you should meditate before bedtime, turning all of your thoughts to the deceased person whom you wish to contact. Talk out loud to his or her spirit and invite it to visit you in a dream. Speak with sincerity and let fear tug not at your heart as you do this, otherwise the spirit will likely pick up these bad vibrations and not appear to you.

Sleeping with a deceased person's photograph next to your bed or with an article of their clothing, or some other personal possession, placed beneath your pillow can also help to bring you into contact with his or her spirit as you sleep and dream.

Ghosts of the Four-Legged Variety

Many of the world religions are of the belief that only human beings possess a soul or a spirit, and that it is not possible for animals to live on after death. I, like many other Witches and other Pagans, believe that animals—if not all living things on Earth—have a spirit that, after the death of the physical body, can choose to move on to eternal rest, reincarnate as either animal or human, or remain earthbound as a ghost.

All one needs to do is look through the many published collections of ghost stories that exist to find that numerous people have had encounters with animals—sometimes a beloved pet that returns from the grave to be with its human master or mistress. Ghostly cats, dogs, horses, and birds are the types of animals most commonly observed in this type of phenomena.

Encounters with animal ghosts are not always accompanied by a materialization of the dead animal's apparition. Frequently, during such encounters, a person may simply sense the animal's presence, feel the animal lick them, brush up against them, or even curl up next to them in bed. Auditory experiences are also common and typically involve a person hearing the animal meowing, purring, or barking; the pitter-patter of paws moving across the floor, a familiar scratching at the door, and so on.

31

Recently, there have been a few psychics who have attracted worldwide attention for their unusual abilities to communicate with the spirits of dead pets and other animals. Many persons consider this to be further proof that animals do in fact possess a spirit or a soul, just as do their human counterparts.

Evil-Natured Ghosts

Just as good and evil exist among the living, they also exist among those in the afterworld. It is said that the spirits of those who are evil in life (such as mass murderers and genocidal leaders like Adolf Hitler) remain so even after their physical bodies die.

There also exist non-human entities (demons) that can be classified as evil. They are said to sometimes appear in the shape of a black-skinned, black-furred, or black-feathered animal—most commonly a dog, cat, goat, hare, or small rodent-like creature. Some paranormal investigators look for the manifestations of ghostly black animals (which are not a  person's or family's deceased pet) as a sign that the situation of a diabolical haunting exists. However, not all hauntings involving spirits in the form of black animals are necessarily of this nature.

The chances of interaction between the living and a true evil spirit—of either the human or non-human variety—are relatively minute. Based on my research, as well as on the personal experiences that others and myself have had with the supernatural, it would appear that the vast majority of hauntings and ghostly sightings are benign in nature. This is not to say that ghosts cannot be frightening or unpleasant.

Earthbound spirits can often be mischievous, taking great delight in scaring us if we allow them to do so. And some spirits, just like some living persons, can be angry or vengeful for various reasons, while others are simply mean because that is the way they are. If we take it upon ourselves to deliberately disturb certain spirits that wish to be left alone, this can also cause them to display a less-than-pleasant disposition or seemingly violent behavior. Nevertheless, very few will truly be evil or demonic. But because many persons find the presence and actions of such spirits to be terrifying or ominous, they automatically and incorrectly assume them to be evil ghosts or demons.

So how, then, does one differentiate between evil and non-evil spirits? This is not always easy to accomplish since both entities can be identical in appearance and mannerism. It would be like trying to discern whom among the living is good or evil simply by their outward appearance or way of speech. The main thing to keep in mind is that the odds of running into a spirit of a true evil or demonic nature are extremely low. Therefore, we should not allow ourselves to become obsessed or overly concerned with them.

For ghost hunters and investigators, observing certain simple precautions—wearing or carrying certain amulets or something made of silver, praying for a blessing or protection from the god or goddess belonging to their particular faith or tradition, or calling upon their guardian angels or spirit guides to be by their sides—normally offers all the protection necessary to ensure their safety in the rare event that they should encounter a bona fide evil spirit or demon.

Is There Anything to Fear?

Many people, both young and old, are afraid of ghosts, although not many will readily admit to such a thing for fear of being labeled superstitious and scorned. Fears that a spirit will cause harm or possession is universal and as old as mankind itself. But perhaps even more terrifying for many non-believers who happen to encounter a ghost is the thought that they might be experiencing hallucinations as a sign of mental illness or a brain tumor. The very idea that one is losing their firm grip on reality can be very alarming to say the least.

Fear is an instinct that nature gave to humans (and animals as well) to give warning when imminent danger is near, but it also manifests itself when we come face-to-face with an unknown or unexplainable situation. However, in nearly all cases of hauntings and spirit encounters, there is absolutely nothing to be feared. Ghosts and spirits, for the most part, are harmless enough, although they *can* frighten some people enough to cause them to injure themselves or even fall victim to heart attacks or psychological disturbances.

How to Rid Yourself of an Unwanted Spirit

If you should suddenly find yourself troubled by an unwelcome spiritual entity, do not allow yourself to become panic-stricken. It is important that you stay calm and rational. Sometimes simply speaking out loud to the spirit and politely asking it to leave you, your family, and your home in peace is all that is necessary to bring the undesired paranormal activity to a halt. Speak in a calm, firm, and respectful manner, employing psychology to help the spirit to move on. Explain to it that it's loved ones are waiting on the other side, by going into the light its sorrow and suffering will end, etc. It is said that many spirits respond well when this type of approach is used.

34

There are also a number of tried-and-true magickal methods available for sending a lingering spirit on its way, many of which can be found in the *Spells and Sorcery* chapter of this book. While anyone can practice magick, regardless of one's cultural or religious background, I strongly suggest to all novices that they acquire at least a basic knowledge of how magick works before engaging in the casting of any spells. Working magick without knowledge of what you're doing can yield dangerous results in a worst-case scenario, or wind up being a complete waste of time and energy on your part at the very least.

But whatever you do, be sure to refrain from shouting at, cursing, or antagonizing the spirit in any way, as this is likely to only upset or anger the spirit, thus worsening the situation for you and any others in your haunted household. Remain positive and do not allow negative thinking and fear to overcome you. And keep in mind that the entity is still a human consciousness (unless it is a non-human spirit, which is another story) and that it possesses the same emotions, moods, and attitudes that it did when alive. There is also a good chance that it may not even be aware that it is dead, or it may simply be afraid of leaving the surroundings that it feels are familiar, safe, and comforting.

If all of your efforts to rid yourself of the spirit by talking to it or by using spellwork fail, do not be tempted to perform an exorcism ritual, especially if you possess no formal training or experience in this area. Exorcism can be an extremely dangerous thing to do, and in most cases serves to only provoke the spirit, thus intensifying the symptoms of the haunting and stirring up, or increasing, poltergeist activity in the home.

Most spirits that exorcisms are attempted upon will naturally respond with hostility and engage in battle with the person or persons trying to drive them out. Very few will ever leave quietly without putting up a fight. Try to see things from the spirit's perspective for a moment. Imagine how you would react if some threatening stranger suddenly barged into your realm of existence, began assaulting you with salt and holy water, cursing at you, and tried to forcibly eject you from your home. You understandably would be frightened, enraged, and forced to defend yourself and the place you call your home in whatever manner you could and by whatever means were available to you. A spirit being forcibly evicted from the place that it considers to be its home will feel and react in precisely the same manner as you.

Keep in mind that most spirits will leave a place only if *they* choose to do so. A human spirit possesses the free will to decide when and where it will go, and although many spirits can be persuaded to leave by spell or spoken word, no person can force them to do something they simply do not wish to do. Also, if your haunting is the type that ghost researchers term a "residual haunting" (a repeated playback of certain past events in the same location at regular or infrequent intervals, and not a haunting involving the conscious energy of a spirit), there really isn't much you or anyone else can do to stop it. Such hauntings usually stop on their own accord and with the passing of time. However, this can often translate to centuries.

If nothing you've tried has worked to make the spirit leave your home, your next step (before calling a real estate agent to sell your house) is to contact a reputable spiritualist medium or your local paranormal researcher or ghost hunters group, many of which can be found in the *Resources* chapter of this book, or on the Internet by using a search engine such as *www.google.com*.

Choose a paranormal investigator carefully just as you would a doctor, an automobile mechanic, or even a contractor for your home. Ghost hunters and researchers come with varying degrees of experience, and from different cultural and religious backgrounds. It is only natural that you will feel more comfortable working with some more than others. It is important that you choose the one that is right for you and for your particular situation.

Most do not charge for their services other than reasonable fees to reimburse their travel expenses to and from the site of the paranormal activity, as well as to cover the cost of such things as supplies (equipment, films, tapes, processing, etc.) Some, especially those affiliated with religious organizations, may also ask for donations. But be leery of those who ask you for large amounts of money up front or who make guarantees that, for a price, they can rid you of your bothersome ghost. In most cases, the only thing such individuals will rid you of is your hard-earned money.

Samhain: Night of the Dead

The Celts of old believed that every year, from sunset on the last night of October until sunset on the first night of November, the invisible veil that separated the mortal world from the spirit world was at its thinnest. This made it the opportune time for the living to communicate with the dead (usually for divinatory purposes) and allowed spirits of the dead to return to earth and walk among the living. Known today as Halloween or All Hallows Eve, this sacred time of the year was known to the ancient Celtic tribes as Samhain (pronounced SOW-en, or SOW-in).

In Ireland, great bonfires would blaze atop hillsides on Samhain to help guide the souls of the dead on their journey to the Celtic underworld, as well as to frighten away any evil ghosts that came to call on the living. It was also customary for offerings of food and drink to be left outside this night to appease not only wandering spirits, but also the fairy folk, who were believed to be out and about at this magickal and mysterious time of the year.

Many of the customs we associate with our relatively modern holiday we call Halloween (jack-o'-lanterns, trick-or-treating, masquerading, bobbing for apples, etc.) can be traced back to centuries-old Celtic practices connected to the rites of Samhain and once used for protection against evil spirits and divining the future.

The Feast of the Hungry Ghosts

According to ancient Chinese folk belief, on the seventh month of the Chinese Lunar Calendar (August, also known as the "Ghost Month") the underworld opens its gates and allows the souls of the dead to wander freely about the Earth and roam the streets of the living for a period of one month.

The 15th day of the seventh month begins an annual Chinese festival called the Feast of the Hungry Ghosts, which lasts for six days. During this colorful and noisy festival, which incorporates the Buddhist ceremony of *putu* (the deliverance of the spirits of the dead), Buddhist and Taoist priests chant liturgies, perform rituals, and burn offerings of incense to the hungry ghosts. Feasts of scrumptious foods are prepared and set out for the wandering souls, and both the living and the dead are entertained by the live performances of street musicians and actors.

Many Chinese families invite their ancestral spirits to join them for a meal, during which joss sticks and daily essentials of paper clothing, shoes, televisions, radios, automobiles, and other luxuries are ritually burned. Such practice is carried out to ensure that the family's present and future generations receive blessings and protection against any imminent harm.

Differing from the Chinese festival of *Oingming*, which is dedicated solely to one's own family and ancestors, the Feast of the Hungry Ghosts is dedicated also to those among the dead who are not one's own ancestors. Its central purpose is to bring peace to the neglected, abandoned, and forgotten dead. Included among this list are those who died without descendents, those who died far away from their loved ones, and those whose lives ended at birth or during childhood. The ghosts of suicide cases and murder victims who never received a proper burial are regarded as the most frightening of all the dead. It is said that, due to their circumstances, they are doomed to eternally haunt the scene of their death, seeking vengeance.

Many people in China regard the Feast of the Hungry Ghosts as an event of great significance, and are most superstitious during this time. Infants and small children will frequently be kept indoors and carefully guarded out of fear that they might be lured away to the dark realms of the underworld by the souls of the restless dead. Evil ghosts are thought to be lurking around every corner, eager to take the lives of young and old alike. It is also thought to be extremely bad luck for anyone to exchange wedding vows or relocate to a new residence during this period. The most unfortunate are said to be the souls of those who happen to die during the Ghost Month, for they will never be able to rest in peace.

On the last day of the Feast of the Hungry Ghosts, a great bonfire is set ablaze, and into its flames are cast paper effigies of ancient deities, special paper currency known as "hell money," and other offerings as a final gift to the dead.

At the midnight hour on the 30th day of the Ghost Month, all wandering souls of the dead return to their place in the underworld and its gates are then closed behind them. There they will remain until the following year when they are once again released for a period of one month.

With a sense of relief and ease, people throughout China return to their normal routine after this period, confident that they have fulfilled their obligations towards their departed ancestors and other souls of the dead.

The Ghost Dance

During a solar eclipse in January of 1889, a Paiute prophet by the name of Wavoka (also known as Jack Wilson) received a mystical vision. While in a state of trance he spoke to God and envisioned a natural catastrophe that would bring about the extinction of the white race, after which the ghosts of all dead Native Americans would return to Earth to co-exist with the living, bringing with them the old way of life that would then last forever. However, in order to bring this into effect, it was necessary for the Native people to chant certain songs and perform an

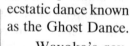

ecstatic dance known as the Ghost Dance.

Wavoka's revelation was the genesis of the short-lived Ghost Dance religious movement that spread among the Plains peoples during the 1880s. It soon took on proportions beyond its original intent, and desperate Native Americans affected by mounting white oppression began dancing and singing the songs that they believed would hasten the end of the threatening white man's culture and the coming of a new world of paradise for the Native Americans. According to author Rosemary Ellen Guiley, "The movement had the greatest effect among the Sioux, a proud and fierce people who had vigorously resisted the whites, most notably in the spectacular defeat of General Custer at Little Big Horn."

It was not uncommon for Ghost Dance ceremonies to last for as long as five days. Those engaged in the shuffling circle dance would enter a trance and then slip into unconsciousness. While in this state they would experience mystical visions of their dead ancestors, a rebirth of the Earth, and a return of the wild buffalo herds to the plains.

While the Ghost Dance inspired unity and fervor among the many Native American tribes that embraced it, it spurred only fear and hysteria among a great number of white settlers, who perceived it as being openly hostile. The United States government responded by outlawing the Ghost Dance from being performed on all reservations. Despite the ban, the Ghost Dances continued, as did the mounting tensions between the whites and the Native Americans, and even between members of the tribes themselves.

In November of 1890, after two Sioux mystics known as Short Bull and Kicking Bear rejected Wavoka's stance on nonviolence and began preaching the elimination of whites, U.S. cavalry soldiers were summoned to the Rosebud and Pine Ridge reservations in South Dakota in an effort to keep the peace. A scuffle broke out and Sitting Bull—a famous and respected Sioux leader, warrior, and medicine man—was killed while resisting arrest. Several of his men also lost their lives that fateful day.

These tragic events ultimately led up to one of the saddest events in American history—the infamous Massacre at Wounded Knee, which occurred on December 29, 1890. The fighting, which lasted for two days, resulted in the deaths of more than 300 hundred men, women, and children, and brought a close to the Ghost Dance religion, as well as the wars on the Western frontier.

Crisis Apparitions and Doppelgangers

Labeled "phantasms of the living" by the British Society for Psychical Research in 1886, crisis apparitions are the apparitions, or so-called "ghosts," of persons who are still alive.

It is not uncommon for crisis apparitions to be spotted in locations that are great distances away from where their living counterparts are. In many cases, the crisis apparition of a person who is in some form of danger, pain, or on the verge of death, will appear to a loved one, whether they be several miles away or on the other side of the world, to make them aware that something is not right. In all cases the person who is in crisis remains completely unaware that they are somehow projecting their own image in this manner. Others may perceive such an image, which is indistinguishable from the real self, either through psychic means (as visions seen in the mind's eye) or through the normal senses.

In some cases, a person will see, or be visited by, his or her own living apparition or double. This type of phenomena is known as a *doppelganger*, which is a German term meaning "double walker." The Swedish term for a person's double is a *vardoger*. Some of its other names include: "beta body," "fluidic body," "pre-physical body," and "subtle body."

Crisis apparitions and doppelgangers present the greatest challenge to science, for they seem to involve a living human being existing in two places simultaneously— a phenomenon known as bi-location. "Bi-location is a concept hardly more congenial to scientists than the idea of returning from the dead," writes Hilary Evans and Patrick Huyghe in *The Field Guide to Ghosts and Other Apparitions*. "But this type of case is entirely compatible with

the widespread belief...that there is a part of us...which can detach from the physical body and for a short while act independently of it." To sum it all up, the projected self can sometimes be made visible to others, at a distance from the physical self.

The phenomenon of crisis apparitions and doppelgangers, of which much has been written and speculated over since the dawn of the spiritualist movement in Victorian times, was well known to the ancients. (The ancient Egyptians, for example, believed that every soul possessed a double, known as a *ka*.) However, the true nature and cause of these remain a mystery in our modern age. One given explanation is that they are projections of a person's astral body. Another is that they are human beings' souls, which are reflections of the physical body.

Eileen J. Garrett, a gifted and renowned medium born in Ireland in the 19th century, viewed a person's double as "a means of telepathic and clairvoyant projection," which could be "manipulated to expand one's consciousness."

But whatever the true nature and cause of this phenomenon may be, many parapsychologists regard crisis

43

apparitions as further proof that there exists a part of living beings capable of exiting the physical body or existing without it that can still communicate with others, accomplish tasks, and function as an independent entity.

From a folkloric viewpoint, legend holds that the appearance of a man's or woman's double is indicative of that individual's imminent demise. In Ireland, a country rich with folklore, hauntings, and mysteries, it is believed by some that if one's double is observed in the morning hours, this means that he or she will live for many years. However, if it is observed in the evening hours, this is a sign of impending death for that individual.

A Witch's double has long been known as a "fetch," and during the Witch-burning era it was commonly believed throughout Europe and New England that a Witch was capable of sending forth his or her fetch to steal, create mischief, or bring harm or death to enemies and rivals. Peasants and royalty alike believed this to be accomplished through the use of special incantations or spells, the aid of the devil, or simply through the power of the Witch's will.

In Search of Ghosts (How to Properly Conduct a Ghost Hunt)

"By and large, it is entirely safe to be a ghost hunter or to become a witness to phenomena of this kind."
—Hans Holzer, *Ghosts*

Some of the most favorable places in which to encounter ghosts and spirits are graveyards, churches, battlefields, old hotels, theatres, schools, historic buildings, and sites where murders, suicides, or fatal accidents are known to have taken place. Many paranormal researchers and spiritualists alike believe that all places where the dead rest—cemeteries, catacombs, mausoleums, ancient burial grounds, etc.—hold the greatest concentration of spirit energy because they are portals to the other side. Another reason is that many earthbound spirits seem, for some reason, to be drawn to their former bodies.

The best times to come face to face with a ghost or spirit while ghost hunting are during the hours between 9 p.m. and 6 a.m., which are known as "the psychic hours." This is not to say that a good ghost hunt cannot be held during daylight hours. However, spirit-photographs taken at night historically have yielded the most favorable results for those on the prowl for disembodied entities.

Always have one or more persons accompany you when hunting for ghosts. Avoid dangerous areas and take care to obey signs warning against trespassing. It is also wise to obtain permission from owners before snooping around on private property with cameras and tape recorders. It is also in your best interest to carry with you some sort of identification bearing your photo in the event that you should be questioned by the police and required to show proof of your identity. Be polite and leave the area at once if asked to do so by a property owner, caretaker, security guard, or police officer. There are plenty of other places in which ghosts and spirits can be found.

Never embark on a ghost hunt without bringing most or all of the following items: a camera containing a fresh roll of 400 or 800 speed 35-millimeter film; a flashlight with extra batteries; notebooks and pencils for documenting all ghostly happenings; a wristwatch for logging in the hour and minute during which events occur; a video camera possessing an infrared feature that enables videotaping in complete darkness; and a tape recorder with high grade tapes for recording spirit voices. More advanced ghost hunters should also bring an E.M.F. detector for reading the electromagnetic fields in a potentially haunted area (levels will typically read higher than normal when ghost or spirit energy is present); a night scope; a battery operated motion detector; a thermometer or thermal scanner for the detection of cold spots; and walkie-talkies if working with a group of others spread out in a large outdoor area or in different rooms of a large building. In the event of an emergency, it is always a good idea to come prepared with a first-aid kit and a cellular phone to use for calling help.

Many ghost hunters feel that it is important to always say a prayer, to whatever deity you have faith in prior to entering a dwelling or area where evil-natured spirits may be lurking. A simple request to one's god or goddess for a blessing or protection is believed by some to allow a person to safely go about his or her business without having to fret about such things as spirit obsession or poltergeist attacks. Carrying magickally-charged amulets, visualizing yourself surrounded by a warm and brilliant white light, and/or wearing the symbol of your faith in silver, whether it be a pentagram, a cross, or a Star of David (also known as the Seal of Solomon), will also help to cast a protective aura around you that evil spirits will not be able to penetrate.

When in search of ghosts and spirits, always do so with an open mind. Any negative feelings transmitted by you or others in your group could very well serve to drive away whatever spirits might be in the area you are combing. At all times be respectful of the dead, never disturb or desecrate their graves, and do not ghost hunt while under the influence of alcohol or drugs. Above all, be prepared for anything and everything!

Be sure to keep a detailed record of all unusual events (including visual sightings, odd sounds and smells, strange feelings, psychic impressions, etc.) that take place during the course of the ghost hunt, regardless of how unimportant they may initially appear. Also note E.M.F. and temperature readings, weather conditions, and the hour and minute when each event happens.

When videotaping or taking pictures at a haunted site, be sure no one is smoking, as cigarette smoke can give the false impression of ectoplasmic mist on the tape or film. A person's breath in cold weather can also be mistaken for a ghostly manifestation in a photo. Keep the lens of your camera clean at all times and do not hesitate to take pictures anywhere and everywhere—especially in areas where you (or someone else) suddenly feel, hear, smell, or see something that appears to be out of the ordinary. If you should happen to observe orbs, mist, or sparkles in your flashes, this indicates that a ghost or spirit is in close range. You should immediately begin taking more pictures in that location.

It is also a good idea, when taking your film in for developing, to request that all pictures on the roll be developed in order to prevent the developer from possibly discarding any blurred, spotted, or streaked photos that he or she might consider to be "bad prints." These types of pictures are often photographic captures of spirit energy.

During audio recording, ask the spirits around you how they died, when they died, and other simple questions. Keep in mind that spirit voices, in most cases, will be inaudible to human ears at the time of recording, but heard (often as faint whispers) when the tape is played back. Be sure to only use a tape recorder with an external microphone, as opposed to one with a built-in microphone, otherwise the sounds of the machine's motors and internal gears will be picked up on the tape, rendering it worthless for your purpose. It is also a good idea to take along spare batteries and tapes.

At the end of the ghost hunt, all persons in the group (if separated) should reunite at a predetermined location at a predetermined time. It is also recommended that, before leaving the area, the spirits there be instructed to stay behind and not follow anyone home. It is a custom among some individuals to conclude a ghost hunt by reciting a special prayer for the spirits of the dead and/or asking the god or goddess of their spiritual tradition to bless and protect them. Some also feel that it is only proper to offer thanks to the spirits for any signs or communications received.

Interview With a Spiritual Medium

I first met Tim Braun on Halloween of 2001 at an occult shop in Hollywood, California called Panpipes Magickal Marketplace. A compassionate and soft-spoken individual, he was born with the rare ability to communicate with the spirits of the dead. In his own words, "My gift, or my forte, is seeing, feeling, and hearing a person who's passed over." Tim believes that the purpose of his gift is to share it with persons who seek answers to life after death, as well as with those desiring to make contact with those who have passed over to the other side. Through his mediumship, he has been instrumental in helping many persons overcome the pain of losing a loved one, as well as providing evidence that the human spirit lives on after the physical body dies.

Born in the Los Angeles suburb of Whittier on December 29, 1969, Tim's special abilities first surfaced at the age of nine when he psychically picked up that his father would develop diabetes in the future, which came to be many years later. It was in his early 20s when he first started seeing spirit images out of the corners of his eyes and hearing spirit voices while standing next to people. These experiences initially caused him understandable concern for the state of his mental health. After being reassured by doctors that there was nothing physically or mentally wrong with him, he soon realized he had a gift and felt that his purpose in this life was to help mankind. About a year later, he began doing mediumistic readings for friends, which became a full-time occupation several years later. According to Tim, "All mediums, like myself, are psychic. But not all psychics are mediums."

In 1995, during his final year at U.S.C. (University of Southern California), Tim Braun experienced a vivid dream, which later proved to be quite prophetic for him. In it he saw himself in Calcutta, India, working with the now-late Mother Teresa. The dream—down to every last detail—came true three months later, signaling to Tim that many great things were yet to come.

Tim recently finished taping 15 episodes of a television show he hosted called *Looking Beyond*, which was aired on Cox Cable in Southern California. The show, which has received good reviews and positive feedback, deals with a wide range of metaphysical subjects, providing viewers with a better understanding of such things as mediumship, astrology, hypnosis, acupuncture, hands on healing, and so forth.

Tim was kind enough to allow me to interview him by telephone. The following are some of the questions I asked him, followed by what he had to say.

49

Q: **Please describe what takes place during one of your sittings with a client.**

A: Prior to a session, I do a two or three minute guided meditation to make the person I'm reading for feel more relaxed, as well as to open my chakras so I can be more psychically alert. I then talk to the client about the sitting and try my best to answer whatever questions they might have about it. It normally takes a few minutes after this before I begin to feel the spirits and see them appear around the person sitting before me. However, with some individuals, I am able to feel and see the spirits of their loved ones during the meditation or immediately following it.

The spirits speak to me telepathically and I pass along to the client everything they tell me. I basically act as a middleman between the spirit and the living. Incidentally, the word "medium" comes from the Latin *medius*, which means, "the middle." If the spirit appears at the left-hand side of the client, this tells me that it is from the mother's side of his or her family. If it appears on their right-hand side, it is from their father's side of the family. But when the spirits appear behind the person, this usually means they are related to neither the mother's side nor father's side of the family. Such a spirit is often a husband, a wife, a son, a daughter, or a friend.

When I feel the energy begin to fade, I'll give the client the opportunity to ask those on the other side a final question before the session ends. After all spirit messages have been given out, I normally do a closing meditation for the client as well as for myself.

Q: **Do you work in a trance state?**

A: I am fully conscious when giving mediumistic readings.

Q: **Do you have any control over which spirits manifest during a sitting?**

A: No. And I believe that any medium that guarantees a client they can bring through a particular spirit is telling a lie.

Q: **Do the spirits that come through during a sitting ever reveal the future?**

A: They frequently speak of persons and events from the past, but they sometimes do make predictions of things to come. If, for instance, the spirits sense that the person, or someone close to them, is soon going to run into trouble or have an accident of some kind, they will issue a warning. If they foresee a death in the near future, they will usually indicate that someone will pass over soon. The exact time of death is not given. I have also had spirits tell clients that there was going to be a birth in the near future, and even accurately predict the sex of the unborn child.

Q: **Have you ever encountered a case of spirit obsession or possession?**

A: No. I've never had that type of encounter, but a friend of mine, who is a hands-on-healer, did. A man from Palm Springs who was dying from cancer had come to him for a session.

This man's friend, who had just passed over, was so much in his aura and in his energy that it was almost like he was possessed by that person. I can't honestly say whether or not he was actually possessed, but after my friend did the healing on this man, the spirit was no longer in his aura.

Q: **Do you also perform spiritual healings?**

A: When a person has a session with a medium such as myself, a lot of healing usually takes place—not only for the person, but for those on the other side as well. So, in this sense, I would answer your question by saying yes.

Q: **Have you or one of your clients ever been harmed by a spirit during a sitting?**

A: No. The spirits come through to give help and guidance. Also, if a spirit desires to make contact through me to the person sitting in front of me, it's going to treat me with respect.

Q: **Do you work with one or more spirit guides?**

A: Yes, I do work with spirit guides. I cannot do this work alone. I would also like to add that everybody, not just mediums, has spirit guides. Usually there are three different guides that will come in and help a person on his or her path. For instance, if you are an actor, you will have a guide that helps you with acting. If you want to be a doctor, you will get someone from the other side that is a medical guide. If you decide to pursue a different profession, a different guide will come to you. It also helps to ask the powers that be to send you someone from the other side that can help you.

Q: **Do you believe in reincarnation?**

A: Yes. It was told to me once that we reincarnate on the average of every 200 years. But recently I was told that this was true for persons of long ago. We now reincarnate much sooner than that because the vibrations of the planet are moving so quickly. I really have no way of proving that though.

Q: **Do you feel that a gift such as yours is something a person has to be born with? Or can anyone learn to develop it?**

A: I really feel that it's something a person has to be born with.

Q: **What advice could you give to a young person who discovers that he or she possesses a gift such as yours?**

A: Meditate in the morning and meditate in the evening. Ask for protection and guidance from whatever Higher Force you believe in. Follow through with your intuitions, give out the messages you receive, be sincere, and never abuse the gift.

Author's note: If you are interested in receiving a reading by telephone, or are in the Los Angeles (Torrance) or Palm Springs areas and would like to arrange for a personal sitting, you may contact Tim Braun by email at: tim@timbraun.net or by telephone at: (626) 308-1614. His Website is: *www.timbraun.net*

A Ghost by Any Other Name

Ghosts have been known by numerous names throughout history and throughout the world. Many of their common and not-so-common names, including some foreign ones, are listed below:

Apparition
Appearance
Bakemono (Japanese)
Bogey
Disembodied spirit
Entity
Espectro (Spanish)
Esprit (French)
Fantasma (Spanish)
Fantome (French)
Gast (Old English)
Geist (German)
Gespenst (German)
Larva (Latin)
Lemures (Latin)
Lau (Andaman Islands)
Manifestation
Obake (Japanese)
Phantasm

Phantom
Poltergeist
Restless dead
Revenant
Shade
Shadow
Specter
Spectral visitor
Spectre (British spelling of Specter)
Spectrum (Latin)
Spettro (Italian)
Spirit
Spook
Vision
Wraith
Youkai (Japanese)
Yuurei (Japanese)

Chapter 2

True Tales of Ghosts and Hauntings

"Ghosts, poltergeists, and haunted houses continually crop up in the news, and the offered explanations that they are mere imagination, or hallucinations, or trickery aren't really convincing."
—Susy Smith, *A Supernatural Primer for the Millions*

The Spirit of Sunnybrae

The green stucco house that stood on Sunnybrae Avenue at times seemed to pulsate with dark and disturbing energies that defied explanation. From the outside, it looked like any other ranch-style house in the San Fernando Valley north of Los Angeles. However, few individuals who stepped foot through its front door into the small foyer that opened on one side to a long narrow corridor eerily illuminated by an old brass and crystal chandelier were able to do so without sensing, or feeling overwhelmed by, a strange and unseen presence.

Many of the people who spent any amount of time in this house felt extremely uncomfortable for no apparent reason, and were anxious to be on their way. Some said they felt as though they were being watched when no one else was around (at least no one who was visible.) And there were even those who felt that the house possessed evil vibrations. One such person, my older cousin Barbara, was of the opinion that the restless spirit that inhabited the house was more than capable of inflicting physical harm.

My mother and I moved into the green house on Sunnybrae in 1980. Before we purchased it, the house was owned by a real estate company and had been turned into a rental property. But for some reason, as I found out from my next-door neighbor who stopped by to welcome us to the neighborhood, few of the past tenants remained in the house for very long. The neighbor was pleased to learn that we had purchased the property and were planning on staying there awhile since there had been so many families moving into the house and then moving out of it within a short period of time. I inquired as to how many people she was talking about, and her reply was that it was well over a dozen in less than two years! This seemed extremely odd as there was nothing noticeably wrong with the house. (In fact, we had just had a building inspector come out and look everything over prior to the closing of the sale and in his written report he gave the house an A+ rating.) The yard was beautifully landscaped with mature palm trees, yuccas, and tall cactus plants, and the backyard boasted a freshly painted in-ground swimming pool. It was an attractive house.

I began to wonder why so many of the people who had lived in the house before me chose not to stay there very long, but could not come up with any reasons. After all, it was a nice house located on a quiet street in a well-kept middle-class neighborhood, and the neighbors that I had met so far all appeared to be very friendly and normal.

Shortly after moving into the house, a series of strange and unexplained events began to take place, starting with a loud and continuous banging sound that awakened us in the middle of the night. Nervously, we went to investigate the sound and found the wooden attic door panel (which was located on the ceiling at the end of the hallway) violently slamming up and down with a great force. It continued on for a few moments as we stood below it and watched in disbelief. And then, as suddenly as it began, it stopped. Before returning to bed, I took a rope and tightly tied one end of it to the handle on the attic door panel and the other to the doorknob of the linen closet below it to prevent the panel from being lifted up again.

The following day, a gentleman who my mother had been dating for the past two years came over to our house and checked out the attic for us. Nothing appeared to be out of the ordinary and he was unable to come up with any explanation for what had taken place the night before. He said if we had our evaporative cooling system on with all of the doors and windows shut, the air pressure might cause the attic door to blow open. However, we had nothing running that night, not even a fan.

One morning after my mother had left the house for work, I awoke to the sound of a loud thud coming from the living room. When I got out of bed to investigate,

I discovered that an oil painting that was hanging over the sofa had fallen down for no apparent reason. I went to re-hang it and noticed that the picture hook was still firmly in place on the wall and the picture wire on the back of the painting was perfectly intact. I puzzled over what could have caused the painting to fall, arriving at the conclusion that someone, or something, had to have lifted the painting's wire up off the picture hook before dropping it onto the sofa. But who? And for what reason?

The spirit that haunted the house on Sunnybrae was becoming more active, and with each passing day I could feel its ominous presence growing stronger. It had made my mother and me aware of it by its poltergeist-like behavior, but it clearly wanted more. It now wanted to reach out and let me know that *it* was aware of *me*.

It accomplished this one afternoon when I was home alone and sitting at the dining room table reading poetry submissions I had received for the *Golden Isis* literary journal that I had recently begun editing and publishing. The house was very still and quiet, except for the ticking of a small porcelain clock in the living room. And then suddenly the silence was broken by the sound of a woman's voice saying my name. The tone of her voice was odd. She had stated my name rather than called it, as though she wanted to make me aware that she knew what my name was. I instinctively looked up, thinking at first that my mother had come home early from work and somehow I didn't hear her come in. I called her name, but a deathly silence was the only reply I received. At this point I became aware of a strange mistiness that seemed to cling to the air. It was very fine and almost undetectable. I began breaking out with goose bumps on my arms and felt an uneasiness enveloping me. I again called out to my mother, asking if she were home. Again there was no reply. I knew it was not my mother. A minute or so passed, and then I heard what sounded like the faint and gentle music of a music box playing in the distance. The melody was unfamiliar to me and I recall that it had a rather melancholy tone. I rose from the table and, with my heart pounding, quietly tiptoed my way across the dining room, through the living room, and down the corridor to my mother's bedroom where the sound of the music seemed to be coming from. But the moment I placed my hand upon the knob of the bedroom door to open it, the music was no more. Like the strange mist in the air, it simply vanished.

Months passed without further incidents. Summer gave way to autumn, and then Thanksgiving arrived, bringing with it a bone-chilling rain. That night we had guests over for dinner—my cousin Barbara, her husband Jimmy, and their two children. They were well aware of the supernatural activity that had taken place in the house earlier in the year, and during our after-dinner conversation, the subject of ghosts somehow came up. Without warning, a loud banging like the sound of an angry fist pounding against the wall thundered from the guest bedroom at the other end of the house. It stopped after a few seconds. Everyone rushed to the room to investigate, but found nothing.

Such events were startling because they happened suddenly and when least expected. But they did not inspire terror within me or make me feel threatened. At least not until the night I was home alone and heard the sound of water being turned on and off from the outdoor faucet on the back of the house. When I looked out the sliding patio door into the moonlit backyard, I was horrified to observe the black silhouette of what appeared to be a man standing in silence and facing the house. The water continued to turn on and off as the figure began walking towards me at a slow pace. With my heart racing a mile a minute, I immediately switched on the lights to the patio and the swimming pool in the hopes of scaring the intruder away, but the intermittent sound of water flowing through the pipes within the walls continued.

For the first time since moving into the house I felt scared to death. I was so terrified that I even phoned the police several times and reported that someone was attempting to break into my house. The police never arrived, and I spent the remainder of that sleepless night in my mother's bedroom, armed with a butcher knife and a hammer, with a heavy chest of drawers barricading the door.

Another frightening incident took place in the house while my mother was away for the weekend with some friends. Barbara and I had made plans to go out that evening to see a movie with her son and daughter, and she had driven her car over to my house to pick me up. Before leaving the house I made sure to turn on a light and a radio (both of which were in the kitchen) so it would give the appearance that someone was at home while I was out. (This was something I always did as a deterrent to burglars.)

Later that evening when we returned to the house, my cousin witnessed a strange shadow move across the drawn shade of the kitchen window as we walked up to the front door. Thinking that it was probably caused by the headlights of a passing car or the reflection of the street light, she quickly dismissed it and didn't even mention it to me until later. I unlocked the front door and we stepped inside the foyer. The house was as silent and cold as a tomb, and the sound of our footsteps on the tiled floor echoed.

"Wasn't the radio playing when we left?" Barbara asked me with a terror-stricken look beginning to appear on her face.

I nervously nodded my head "yes" as I went into the kitchen to examine the radio, only to find that someone, or something, had turned the knob to the off position. I suddenly felt an awareness of a strange and threatening presence in the house, and despite the chill in the air, I could feel myself breaking out in a cold sweat.

"You didn't leave a candle burning in one of the bedrooms, did you?" I heard Barbara ask from the foyer, where she was still standing.

"No, of course not." I replied as I quickly returned to the foyer to see what she was referring to. I could see a strange light emanating from one of the bedrooms at the end of the corridor. It was like the soft glow given off by a candle, a small kerosene lamp, or perhaps a night-light. We stood there for about half a minute with our eyes fixed upon it, when all of a sudden the glow was eclipsed by the dark shadow of a human-shaped figure moving towards us. We screamed and, without hesitation, ran from the house as fast as our legs could carry us, taking refuge in Barbara's car, which was parked alongside the curb in front of the house. We locked the doors, started up the engine, and then sat there for what seemed to be an eternity, observing the house for any sign of movement or activity coming from within. There was none.

We finally drove over to the apartment complex where my mother was and told her what we had just experienced back at Sunnybrae. She rounded up her friends and we all returned to the house, only to find everything looking quite normal. All the rooms were carefully checked, but there were no signs of a break-in and nothing was missing. I noticed the odd chill that we had felt inside the house earlier was now gone.

Around this time, Barbara was beginning to experience weird and horrible visions about my house. One time she saw in her mind's eye one of my living room walls (the one that the painting had fallen down from) covered in blood, and she picked up what she felt to be psychic impressions of a middle-aged woman being brutally murdered in the house. She also felt that the ghosts of both the slain woman and her killer haunted the house.

Whether Barbara's visions were of actual events of the past that had taken place in the house or merely the result of fear and an overactive imagination, they prompted me nevertheless to begin researching the history of the house in the hopes that I might find some answers. I began by interviewing some of the neighbors to find out if they knew of any deaths or murders that had taken place in the house. No one I spoke to had knowledge of any such events. But then none of them had lived in the neighborhood long enough to know the complete history of the house and all who had occupied it before my mother and me.

My next step was to go to the public library and look through their newspaper archives in the hopes of finding some information. Hours upon hours were spent scouring through obituaries and hunting for news articles on West Valley murders and missing persons, but all of my efforts proved to be fruitless. Feeling as though I were attempting to find the elusive needle in a haystack, I decided to give up and returned home frustrated and mentally exhausted.

It now seemed that the only way left to discover what had really happened in the house, who was haunting it and why, was to hold a séance. However, I was unable to find any persons willing (or perhaps brave enough) to attend. And I certainly did not feel at all comfortable with the idea of trying to make contact by myself with whatever it was that lurked in the shadows of Sunnybrae.

My research of the house's haunted history had come to an end, but the hauntings themselves did not. In fact, they were becoming more frequent...and more terrifying!

One evening the light fixture on my mother's bedroom ceiling mysteriously exploded, sending a shower of sparks down upon the bed where my mother was sleeping. Shortly after that my cousin Barbara reported to me that several times after phoning me and reaching my answering machine she would hear a strange man's voice whispering something on the line while she was attempting to leave a message for me. The man's voice was not heard when the tape was played back.

These unexplained happenings and the unsettling atmosphere within the house were beginning to have a negative effect upon both my mother and myself. My mother seemed to be undergoing a personality change. She was becoming increasingly irritable and at times her behavior could be described as being next to irrational. It was as though she were slowly transforming into a totally different person than the mother I had known and loved all my life, which greatly disturbed me. I, on the other hand, found myself slowly sinking into a state of depression for no apparent reason. I started writing morbid poetry about death, blood-drinking vampire lovers, and being buried alive. A growing interest in the darker side of the occult also began to consume me.

Of the many death-oriented poems I penned while living in the house on Sunnybrae Avenue, the one I wrote about premature burial was particularly haunting for me. Inspired by a story written by Edgar Allan Poe, the following poem was first published in *Golden Isis Magazine* in 1980, and reprinted (in a slightly modified version) in the July 1987 issue of *Thirteen*:

Premature Burial

Black umbrellas under the rain,
Tears are shed, sympathy exchanged.
Mourners hide their faces pale,
Draped in black lace veils.
The lid is closed, the casket lowered,
Prayers fall on deaf ears,
As to the womb of Mother Earth
My ashes are returned.
But in the rumble of the thunder
And the silence of the dirt,
Where flesh does rot and maggots feed,
My screams remain unheard.

Events unrelated to the haunting forced us to put the house on Sunnybrae Avenue up for sale in 1982. However, selling it proved to be no easy task. Many prospective buyers came to look at the place, but it seemed that no one wanted to make us any offers. Not surprisingly, I heard more than one person comment that the house "just didn't feel right." I remember a young Hispanic couple that my realtor brought over to look at the house. They did a quick walk-through and from the other room I overheard the wife saying that she did not like the house and wanted to leave right away. She then said something in Spanish to her husband, her sentence ending with the words, "Dracula's castle."

We eventually sold the house, but it was not until we reduced the asking price to several thousand dollars below what we had bought it for two years prior that any buyer would make us an offer. We were displeased to lose money on our investment, but at the same time happy to be rid of it and all of its negative energy.

Two days before Friday the 13th in August of 1982, we moved our belongings out of the house. As my mother and I walked to the car with our luggage in hand, I turned around to take one final look at what had become our former home. I suddenly felt a sense of liberation and relief sweep through me, as though some dark cloud had finally been lifted. From that day forward, my mother returned to being her old self, and my bouts with depression ended, as did my strange obsession with death and the dark side.

The Moses Day Homestead

On busy Boston Road in Haverhill, Massachusetts, there stands a stately, 12-room, late 17th century Colonial house known to the local Historical Society as the Moses Day Homestead. It is one of the oldest homes in the area, but for four years it was a home I shared with Al (my significant other), my mother, and my Uncle Richard, who was severely afflicted by Parkinson's disease.

On the day that I purchased the property, my real estate agent, who claimed to have seen the fleeting image of a Colonial-era ghost in a rocking chair next to the master bedroom fireplace while showing the house to another prospective buyer, presented me with a housewarming present. It was a beautifully bound research paper done by a local historian who painstakingly chronicled the history of the Moses Day Homestead, listing the names of all persons known to have lived in the house over the past 300 years. It also included the dates of their births and deaths.

While browsing through the numerous names of the house's former occupants, I couldn't help but wonder to myself if the spirits of any of these persons might still be inhabiting the house.

It wasn't long after the move into our new home that a series of unusual and unexplained events began to unfold. For some reason, many of them took place in the master bedroom, where Al and I slept.

Late one night, the mournful sound of a child softly sobbing disturbed our sleep. It seemed to be emanating from within the master bedroom fireplace, which, like the other six fireplaces in the house, had been sealed up with bricks for an untold number of years. Al and I heard this eerie crying on numerous occasions, although it always happened late at night and seemed to wait until after we had fallen asleep. Sometimes, instead of the crying, we would hear a whispering voice coming from the fireplace, but no matter how carefully we listened, we could never make out clearly what it was saying.

The mystery of the haunted master bedroom fireplace fired our imaginations and prompted us one day to break it open with a sledgehammer to reveal whatever dark and perhaps centuries-old secrets might be within. After knocking down the bricks and looking inside, our eyes were met by a two-foot deep pile of ashes, chimney soot, and broken creosote-covered bricks enshrouded by cobwebs that were thick and gray with decades of accumulated dust. Using a shovel, we began cleaning out the fireplace and were quite aghast when we happened upon a large bone amidst the debris. We initially thought it to be a human bone, but later learned that it was actually the hind leg bone of a large dog.

But this only added more questions to the mystery. Where was the rest of the dog's skeleton? For what reason was one of its bones sealed up long ago in the master bed-room fireplace? And was the ghostly crying we frequently heard at night perhaps from a long-dead ghostly child mourning the loss of a beloved pet from so very long ago? One can only wonder.

Al and I frequently heard at night what appeared to be the sound of footsteps coming from the attic above our master bedroom, and one afternoon while Al was helping me to put away some clean laundry, an upright vacuum cleaner on the other side of the room suddenly switched on by itself, startling the daylights out of us, to say the least!

One night while I was sleeping in the master bedroom, I experienced a very unusual and frightening dream. It was the sort of dream that feels so real that you can't help but wonder if it is more than a mere dream. In my particu-lar case, I felt that something supernatural was using my dream as a means to communicate with me: I dreamt that I woke up to find myself alone in the bedroom. I got out of bed and went downstairs to the living room. The televi-sion set was on but there was no volume, and, in front of it, I saw Al supine and levitating in the air in some sort of a trance state with his eyes wide open. As if someone else were controlling my every move, I began walking to the kitchen, where, in the dark, I could see some black shape-less thing materialize and then begin to slowly move in my direction. Gripped by terror, I let out a scream and then awoke from the dream.

As in the dream, I found myself alone in the bedroom. I went downstairs to find Al and from the hallway at the bottom of the stairs I could see the light from the televi-sion coming from the living room, but there was no sound. The volume had either been turned completely off or down so low that it was barely audible. Feeling a bit uneasy because of the similarities between what I had just experienced in the dream state and what I was now experiencing in the waking state, I entered the living room, not knowing what to expect. I found Al on the floor in front of the television set. He was asleep and his body was in a supine position. I then heard a strange noise come from within the kitchen and contemplated investigating it. However, my fear of re-encountering the black shapeless entity I had seen earlier in my dream was far greater than my curiosity, so, instead, I roused Al from his sleep and had him follow me back upstairs to bed.

The following year, as my Uncle Richard's condition worsened and he began to grow more frail and weak, a rash of poltergeist-like activity began to break out in his bedroom. Baskets of laundry would be overturned onto the floor and heavy drawers filled with clothes would be found out of the dresser and stacked on the floor at the opposite side of the room. A small hole appeared on the wall and, as though being slowly chipped away at, began to increase in size with each passing day until it was around twelve inches in diameter. Bedridden and increasingly delirious, Uncle Richard did not possess the strength to carry out such actions.

He began to see strange people in his room when no one other than himself was there. And one time he angrily demanded that my mother tell him who all these people were and why they kept entering his room at night and waking him up. He told her that they would whisper and mumble strange things to him in an unintelligible manner. My mother thought him mad.

At night we could all hear him inside his bedroom at the top of the stairs conversing with his phantom visitors. Sometimes he would engage in lengthy conversations with them, telling jokes and laughing. And sometimes it sounded to us as though he were speaking backwards or in some unrecognizable foreign language, which is said to be one of the common characteristics of the possessed. At times he would become quite incensed and order them to get out of his room. One time we overheard him engaging in a conversation with his mother, who had been dead for the past 15 years.

As death drew nearer to him, Uncle Richard's mental state began to deteriorate rapidly, leaving the rest of us unsure if the nocturnal visitations he claimed to be experiencing were nothing more than the result of dementia brought on by his failing health, or if they were actually spirits of the dead coming to call on him. After all, we *were* living in a house where paranormal phenomena had been experienced at one time or another by all members of the household.

But, undoubtedly, one of the weirdest and most spine-chilling things we experienced with my uncle was the night my mother, Al, and I overheard him alone in his bedroom speaking in multiple voices, including one that sounded like a woman's. Intrigued, the three of us stood at the bottom of the stairs for quite some time and listened intently to the bizarre and unintelligible rambling taking place in the darkness behind his bedroom door. However, when the voices began to talk *simultaneously*, we turned and looked at each other with horror and bewilderment etched upon our faces. Al made the suggestion that we go upstairs and check on Richard, but none of us felt very comfortable doing that at this point. After the bizarre gibberish from the room upstairs gave way to an eerie silence, the three of us mustered up enough nerve to tiptoe into it with a flashlight. We found Uncle Richard in bed and sleeping soundly. We checked around, but nothing in the room appeared to be disturbed.

The following evening when I went to give Uncle Richard his medication, I discovered him lying on his bed with his eyes staring lifelessly and his mouth open and frightfully contorted. His flesh was discolored and cold, and I knew immediately that he was dead. The expression on his face was dreadful. He looked as though something had literally scared him to death.

We had Uncle Richard's body cremated, and his ashes were returned to us in a small cremation box, which I placed upon my altar in the attic and said a blessing over.

Not long after his death, my mother had a frightening experience in her bedroom. She awoke one night to find an old piece of yellowed and decomposing lace draped across her throat. When she showed it to me the following morning, I received from it a psychic impression that it had come from the burial shroud of a corpse. I also felt that the corpse was someone who had lived in the house a very long time ago, but whose spirit remained. How or why the piece of lace came to appear in my mother's bedroom we will probably never know.

Al was also targeted on a number of occasions by the restless dead of the Moses Day Homestead. One afternoon, while mowing the back lawn, he was pelted by several glass bottles and empty soft drink cans thrown by unseen forces. Another time, while raking leaves on the south side of the house, a screen from one of the upstairs windows came loose and plummeted to the ground, nearly hitting him on the head. However, these unexplained "attacks" and other ones similar to them never scared Al all that much. Instead, he found such phenomenon to be highly fascinating and, even at times, rather amusing.

One evening while my mother and I were in the kitchen quarreling over something, we were interrupted by a loud, rapid succession of poundings. It seemed to be coming from up in the attic, where we were storing Uncle Richard's cremation box until deciding upon which course of action to take with it. We ascended to the top of the attic stairs to investigate, but could find no explanation for the poundings. We wondered if it could have been a sign that Richard's spirit was disturbed by our quarreling, or perhaps he was trying to tell us that he was not at rest due to his cremated remains being left in the attic.

The following spring, we buried Richard's ashes in an unmarked grave on the grounds, and a feeling of calm seemed to come over the entire house. We felt in our hearts that Richard's spirit was finally able to rest in peace.

In December of 1990, we sold the old Moses Day Homestead and moved back to the San Fernando Valley north of Los Angeles. We stayed there for three years until I experienced a disturbing premonition that prompted us to move back East. Approximately three weeks after leaving California, a devastating earthquake struck the San Fernando Valley, registering 6.7 on the Richter scale.

> "In almost every family there is a record how some one has 'heard a voice they cannot hear,' or the dead speaking in the familiar tones. Hence the belief in ghosts, as soon as men began to care for death at all, or to miss those who had gone." —Charles Godfrey Leland

The Haunting of Dunwich Manor

Perched grandly atop a hill surrounded by two acres of wooded grounds near the Canadian border in upstate New York, the Victorian mansion that eventually came to be known to those in my coven as "Dunwich Manor"

71

seemed to cast a spell of Victorian elegance and cobwebbed secrets over me from the first moment I laid eyes upon it. Weathered by more than a century's worth of summer storms and brutal winters, the house was in need of some tender loving care. Behind it stood a long two-story carriage house that was far older than the main house and somewhat in a state of disrepair.

The carriage house was rumored to possess a secret underground passageway that was used by black slaves escaping to Canada back in the days of the so-called "Underground Railroad." Atop its roof, the rusted blades of an old fan shrieked eerily in the chilly breezes that heralded the approach of an early and bitter cold winter.

Built in the latter part of the 19th century by Edwin Richardson (one of a group of men brought to the area by  the building of the railroad), the house was locally famous for being the first in the rural community of Fort Covington to utilize furnace heating, and had once been regarded as one of the finest properties in all of Franklin County. But the house, I later learned, had a widespread reputation for being haunted and many of the townsfolk were scared to step foot inside of it, let alone even come near the place—especially after sundown. There were reports of many a passerby claiming to hear the sounds of crying coming from the attic late at night, strange lights glowing and moving in the windows when no one was at home, and other strange tales.

Even those among the few who were unfamiliar with any of the local legends surrounding the old Victorian on the hill could hardly gaze upon the place without sensing that there was a ghostly presence in and around the house and its grounds. Especially in its present condition, it looked every bit like a classic haunted mansion straight out of a Hollywood horror film. Yet, in spite of its faded peeling paint and sagging front porch, I looked upon the house as truly a beautiful work of art that retained much of its graceful charm from the days of yesteryear. I had always dreamed of buying and living in an old Victorian house, and now my lifelong dream was about to be realized.

Gazing up at one of the attic windows I was almost sure I had seen the face of a pale woman peering out from behind the clouded panes of glass. But no sooner had my eyes begun to focus upon her she was gone. As the real estate agent unlocked the back door to take us inside for a tour of the house, I half-jokingly asked her if the house had any ghosts. She smiled at me and said, "The current owners haven't mentioned anything to me about the house being haunted...but you never know! Plenty of people around these parts are under the impression that it is."

She went on to inform me that if the owners had indicated anything to her about the house being haunted, under some New York real estate law she would be legally obligated to disclose such information to all prospective buyers. She then began telling me a true and interesting story about a person who had recently purchased an old and rather expensive riverfront Victorian house in Nyack, New York, and then found out later, when a ghost-fearing architect refused to do any work on the house, that the place was frequently visited by an apparition dressed in clothing of the Revolutionary War era. The apparition was said to be benevolent by nature; however, the buyer went to court just the same to seek rescission of the sale based on the grounds that the house had a ghost. Because neither the owners nor the real estate agent prior to the sale had made any mention of the well-known hauntings (which had been documented in an article appearing in the *Reader's*

Digest in 1991), the judge awarded the case to the buyer and ordered that his down payment be returned!

"I would never do such a thing," I told the real estate agent as she lead me through a pair of recessed paneled pocket doors into the grand parlor with its ornate plaster moldings and trio of tall stately windows. "I've always found ghosts and haunted houses to be absolutely intriguing."

As I followed her up a winding staircase past an exquisite leaded stained-glass window befitting a house of worship, she said to me, almost in a whisper, "I'm sure then that you'll find this house to be very interesting. That is, of course, if you decide later to purchase it."

And purchase it is exactly what I ended up doing. In December of 1993 the closing papers were signed, sealed and delivered, and I, along with Al and my dear old mother, packed up our belongings and moved into the house.

The ghosts that haunted our old "painted lady" (as Victorian houses are so romantically nicknamed) wasted little time in making their presence known to us. The moving van with our furniture had not yet arrived so we spent our first night in the house sleeping in the living room on an old sofabed that the previous owners had left behind. It was shortly after midnight when I awoke from my sleep to hear the sound of creaking floorboards coming form the rooms above us. Terrified that someone had broken into the house while we were asleep and was prowling around on the second floor, I woke Al from his sleep and told him I thought there was a prowler in the house. He went to investigate but returned minutes later and informed me that there was nobody upstairs, reassuring me that the house was quite secure. He suggested that the creaks I had heard was probably the house settling, which is hardly uncommon among many old houses. He then added, "It's either that or there's a ghost walking around upstairs."

We shut off the old Capo di Monte chandelier that hung from an ornate plaster medallion in the center of the ceiling and returned to bed. Not more than a few minutes had passed before the temperature in the house suddenly grew strangely cold. As I was thinking to myself how strange this was, being that the furnace was running and the old steam radiators in every room were scorching hot to the touch, the silence of the dark night was abruptly shattered by a loud banging coming from the second floor. It sounded like a fist pounding angrily upon a wall and slowly traveled from the east end of the house towards the west end, where the winding staircase was. I stood at the bottom of the stairs and bravely shouted up at the darkness above me, "Stop that racket up there! We're trying to get some sleep down here!" The sound immediately ceased as my words echoed through the empty rooms and I could feel the warmth of the radiators returning to the house.

From that moment forward I was convinced that we were not alone in that house. I felt I had made contact that night with a spirit. It had heard my voice, and it was aware of my presence in the house (or perhaps I should say, it was aware of my presence in what it felt was *its* house). The thought of this excited me greatly, but at the same time left me with a creepy feeling that covered me from head to toe in the way that a spider spins its silky threads of death around the body of an insect trapped in its web.

Shortly after moving into the house we began to do some renovation and remodeling work. With our master bedroom being the first project on the list, Al and I had to move our bed and dresser into a small guest room near the top of the stairs, which we slept in until the work in the master bedroom had been completed.

75

The guest bedroom was a cape-styled room with a cracked and water-damaged plaster ceiling, a beige formal-design wallpaper that had seen better days, deteriorating gold brocade draperies that had lost their elegance to the ravages of time, and a cobwebbed hanging light with a bell-shaped glass shade that was considered modern around the turn of the last century. But the room also had a certain unexplainable strangeness and sadness about it that I did not sense as strongly in any of the other rooms in the house, except for a small junk-filled "sewing room" in the attic that oddly had a padlocked door. (According to local legend, in the previous century a woman afflicted by mental illness had been kept locked away in the attic, where she eventually met her death. Upon opening the padlocked room in the attic we found the walls and ceiling to be covered by a green chalk-like substance, which, when scrubbed off with soap and water, revealed several blood-stained handprints that had turned brown with age.)

The first night Al and I slept in the guest bedroom, I had an odd and terrifying experience, which continues to this very day to give me the chills when my memory reels back to it. I dreamt that I awoke in the middle of the night and sat up in bed. A hazy pale light, which could have been generated by either a streetlight or the moon, was peeking through a slit between the drapery panels and illuminating the room just enough that I could make out the wall facing the foot of my bed. I became aware of a door in the center of the wall where no door had been before and it began to open slowly and without making the slightest sound. I remember this striking me as quite a curious thing as there were no other rooms on the other side of that wall. There was nothing but the outside. After the door had opened all the way, the ominous figure of a faceless man in black appeared in the doorway and extended one of his hands to me. I felt myself starting to reach out to take his hand when all of a sudden something told me that if I touched him I would surely die. I immediately pulled my hand back and screamed "No!" as loud as my lungs would allow me to. He instantly retreated and the door slammed shut behind him.

With my heart racing and my body damp from my cold sweat, I then awoke from what I had perceived to be a horrifying nightmare. As I sat up and looked at the wall facing me, relieved to see only the faded beige wallpaper that was slightly curling at the seams, Al also awoke and sat up next to me. Assuming that I had awakened him by screaming in my sleep, I explained that I had just experienced a nightmare and, without going into any of the details of the dream, apologized for waking him up.

But Al had not heard me scream. Something else was responsible for startling him from his sleep. I asked him what it was then that caused him to wake up, instantly feeling the cold chill of goose bumps creep across my flesh when I heard him reply that it was the loud and unmistakable sound of a slamming door.

It was in the spring after the winter snows had finally melted away that our friend Lisa drove out from Boston to visit us for a few days. We put her up in the guest bedroom (which by now had been redecorated) and felt it best not to mention the weird dream that Al and I had experienced while sleeping in that room. It wasn't that we thought she would be scared by it. Rather, it was because we didn't think she would be open to it. When it came to matters of the supernatural, Lisa was skeptical by nature and hardly a believer in ghosts or anything of that sort. She had known for many years of my interest in, and practice of, Witchcraft and the occult arts, and not only accepted them, but respected my ways and beliefs even though they were much different than hers. Yet at the same time she prided herself as being the type of person who firmly believed that all things, no matter how strange and mystifying they may seem, had to have a logical or scientific explanation. To our friend from Boston, the idea of ghosts was neither logical nor scientific. It was next to being downright ludicrous.

Our visit with Lisa seemed to be going very well. However, I couldn't help but notice that for the first two days she stayed with us, her bedroom light burned continuously throughout the night. Our bedroom doors had glass transom windows above them that allowed her light to penetrate into our room, making it difficult for Al and me to get a restful night's sleep. During breakfast on the third day of her visit I politely asked if she was having some trouble sleeping or if she was always in the habit of sleeping with a light on.

Much to my surprise, Lisa suddenly became very emotionally distraught and, with tears glistening in her eyes, began telling me of a man in black and a woman in a Victorian-era dress who had been appearing in her room for the past two nights, scaring and even physically assaulting her. She was afraid to mention anything to us for fear that we wouldn't believe her, or worse, that we would think she was fabricating the story or maybe had taken leave of her senses. She admitted that she initially thought Al and I had entered her room and, under the cover of darkness, were playing a mean joke on her to scare her or try to make her believe in ghosts. She soon realized that it was not us in her room and returned to sleep, passing the experience off as nothing more than a bizarre dream, brought on perhaps by the creepy atmosphere of the house and the antique Victorian furniture that filled it. However, the man and woman appeared in her room once again. This time the woman placed her hands over Lisa's throat and, according to Lisa, tried to choke her while the man in black stood silently at the other side of the bed and looked on. During her struggle, Lisa managed to switch on the lamp on the table next to the bed, which caused her unwelcome visitors to instantly vanish. Shaken and unable to return to sleep, she stayed up for the remainder of the night and passed away the hours reading a book.

The following night, after turning off her bedroom light and drifting off to sleep, the phantom couple again invaded the darkness of Lisa's room. This time the man held Lisa down on the bed while the woman in the Victorian dress pulled violently on one of her arms as if to dislocate it from its socket. The experience was terrifying for her and she found that the only way to keep her attackers at bay was to keep the light on until the first light of dawn appeared at the window.

As our friend enumerated her story to us, it was clear that she was visibly shaken by what had been taking place in her room. I tried to reassure her that they were nothing more than recurring nightmares. But Lisa felt sure that she was not sleeping at the time of the attacks. She was fully awake.

At this point I decided to tell our houseguest about my strange dream about the man in black and the sound of the slamming door in my dream that woke up Al when we were occupying the guest room. Lisa and I both felt that there was a definite connection between the man in my dream and the one who was appearing in her room. I suggested that we perform a banishing ritual in the bedroom to clear it of any and all evil spirits, and was a bit taken aback when Lisa indicated that she supported the idea. I was even more surprised when she asked if she could participate in it. Al and I saw no reason why she shouldn't.

That evening, after the sun had disappeared below the western horizon and the sky over our house swarmed with its nightly bats, I sprinkled some salt upon the floor in the guest bedroom and fumigated the room with a burning smudge bundle made from sage and cedar (two herbs long reputed to possess protective powers and long used by Witches and shamans to banish evil spirits and negative energies). I then cast a circle of protection on the floor, in which Lisa, Al, and myself stood, and lit four white pillar candles—one at each of the four directional points along the circumference of the circle. As the fragrant smoke and candle glow filled the room, I invoked the Goddess and Horned God with a prayer and asked for their protection during and after the ritual. I then proceeded to intone an incantation adapted from one found in an old Sybil Leek book called *Driving Out the Devils*:

> "In the name of the Mother Goddess!
>
> I cast you out, all evil spirits!
>
> In the name of Diana, depart!
>
> In the name of Astarte, depart!
>
> In the name of Lilith, depart!
>
> In the name of Bridget, depart!
>
> In the name of all good creatures,
>
> Leave this house! Leave this house!
>
> Leave this house! Leave this house!
>
> This place is our domain,
>
> And we are stronger than you!
>
> Depart, all evil spirits!
>
> Depart from this house at once!"

As I repeated the incantation over and over again, I noticed the flames of the candles flickering wildly and burning higher than I had ever seen before—at least six inches, if not more! A cold chill swept through the room as the walls began to creak and the glass panes of the windows rattled. After awhile, the creaks and rattling subsided and an air of tranquility came over the room. I looked down at the candles around the circle and their flames burned once again at a normal rate. The dark presence each of us had felt before in the room was no longer around and I was confident that the ritual had been successful in driving out whatever evil spirits had once occupied this part of the house.

That night, Lisa slept in the guest room undisturbed and without the need to keep the light on. However, the following morning at the breakfast table my mother began to mention how she awoke in the middle of the night to find a woman standing in the doorway leading to her bedroom. The room was dark and she was unable to clearly make out the woman's face. However, the woman appeared to be about the same height as Lisa (who is considerably shorter than I am), so my mother assumed that's who it was.

"If you're too scared to sleep by yourself, Lisa, you're welcome to share the bed with me," whispered my mother, aware of the disturbing nightmares (or whatever they were) that had been plaguing Lisa's sleep since she arrived at our house.

The woman did not reply. A few moments passed and then she disappeared into the darkness of the hallway. My mother turned over with her back facing the door and began to drift into a light sleep when all of a sudden she felt the other side of her mattress sinking down as though from the weight of a person's body. Assuming Lisa had reconsidered her offer to join her, she said nothing and returned off to sleep.

Lisa stared at my mother with a look of shock upon her face. "But I didn't sleep in your bedroom last night," she stated, "I slept by myself in the guest room the whole night."

At first my mother thought that Lisa was playing some sort of a joke on her, but when she realized that no joke was being carried out, she turned to me with a concerned look upon her face and asked, "Then who, or what, was sleeping in bed with me last night?" It was a question that to this very day remains unanswered.

In October of the following year, Lisa drove out to upstate New York for another visit, this time to spend Halloween with us. The spirits of the house were kinder to her this time and no terrifying nightmares or ghostly attacks had befallen her while sleeping in the now infamous guest room. But her second visit was not to be without a few unsettling disturbances that defied explanation.

One of the previous owners of the house—a woman known as Hattie—had purchased the property on a Halloween more than a half century earlier and was reputed to have been a Witch. She was also buried in the town cemetery out on Route 37 not more than a mile away. During a discussion of Hattie, Lisa and I began to wonder if she could be one of the spirits haunting the house, or if she might know (or be willing to tell us) the identities of those who were and for what reason they were still here. Being that it was a Halloween night—a time when the veil between the world of the living and the world of spirits is said to be at its thinnest—we felt that it was the opportune time to pay old Hattie a visit.

Lisa, Al, and I drove out to the deserted cemetery and searched with a flashlight for Hattie's grave. After locating it, I placed a Halloween candle in the shape of a ghost upon her grave marker and lit it with a match. The three of us stood in a circle around the grave as I called out to Hattie, inviting her spirit to appear before us or to use one of us as a medium through which to speak. We waited for the sound of a voice or some sort of sign that she was with us, but all that replied was the whistling of the wind through the bare trees and the scraping sound of crisp autumn leaves blowing across the pavement of the graveyard road.

We tried again to make contact with Hattie's spirit. This time I placed the palms of my hands upon her stone grave marker and called her name three times. Lisa whispered that she felt someone watching us, even though there was no visible sign of anyone else in the cemetery other than the three of us. Al agreed with her, and I was feeling it very strongly myself. Suddenly the gravestone upon which my hands were resting began to move slowly rotating in a clockwise manner. The flame of the ghost candle went out and then a small rock appeared out of nowhere and loudly struck the side of Lisa's car, which was parked less than 10 feet away from us. At that point we unanimously agreed that is was time to return home. As we drove towards the old gates of the cemetery, my mind suddenly flashed back to the graveyard scene from George Romero's classic horror film, *The Night of the Living Dead*, which had terrified me as a young teenager.

After arriving back at our house, Al went inside to get ready for bed while Lisa and I strolled around the moonlit grounds discussing the bizarre events of that evening. Lisa had never before experienced anything quite like that in her life and she confided to me that she could no longer be 100 percent sure that ghosts were merely figments of the imagination. Our walk lead us to the old carriage house and, as we neared the building, Lisa gazed up at one of the second story windows and said that she sensed something was up there—something not of flesh and blood—and asked me if I could feel it too. I looked up at the window and although I could see no one, I couldn't help but get the distinct feeling that someone or something was indeed up there, watching us, perhaps even waiting for us. A chilling thought crossed my mind: *Could something supernatural have followed us home from the cemetery?*

At that instant, a cold gust of wind howled through the carriage house and, with a loud heart-stopping boom that sounded like the firing of a canon, the entire windowpane of the window we were staring at blew out from its wooden frame and hurled to the ground in our direction. Lisa and I screamed and ran back to the house as fast as humanly possible. Lisa decided to return home to Boston the next day, and, although we remained good friends, she never visited us in Fort Covington again.

On Candlemas of 1996, Coven Mandragora was officially established and I was elected to serve as its High Priestess. Dunwich Manor soon became its covenstead with nearly every one of our coven meetings and sabbat rituals being held there throughout the following two years.

During one of our open circles held at my house, a young gentlemen who came as a guest of one of my coven members became extremely unglued when he experienced the sensation of a cold and invisible hand touching his arm while sitting in the parlor. This individual apparently had a great fear of the supernatural for he lurched from his chair, frantically shouting that a ghost had touched him. Before I, or anyone else, could say two words, he was out the back door and on his way home (or perhaps to the nearest bar)!

One night a few close members of the coven and I went up to the attic to hold a séance. About halfway up the stairs leading to the attic, Marlene was suddenly overwhelmed by a strong energy that filled her with great sadness and brought tears to her eyes. Her body grew weak as though all of her physical strength had been drained form her, and we had to assist her in climbing the rest of the way up the stairs.

Drawn to an old wicker rocking chair near the east-facing window of the attic, Marlene said that she felt around her the "grandmotherly presence" of a female spirit—perhaps that of Hattie—who liked to sit in the rocker and gaze out at the garden below. She was a benevolent spirit and a matriarch of the house, according to Marlene's psychic impressions. However, there were other spirits inhabiting the house…and not all of them benevolent. One, in particular, was a "man with a black aura" who Marlene sensed was extremely evil. But she also felt that the protective matriarchal spirit that watched over the house and all in it kept us safe from his clutches.

We proceeded to enter the small south-facing room with the padlocked door and sat down on the floor to form a circle around a burning candle. Joining hands, we all gazed into the glow of the candle's flickering flame. I called out to the spirits: "Is anybody here with us? Is there anyone out there who wishes to communicate? If there is, please feel free to speak through one of us, or simply give us some kind of sign that you're here."

The room began to grow colder and then several loud creaks were heard coming from the wall behind me. Minutes passed before I felt myself falling into a trance. But it was unlike any of the other trances I had experienced during séances in the past. I kept slipping in and out of the trance state; my mind reeling with bizarre disconnected thoughts that came through like static on a radio. Soon my heart was overcome by a torrent of mixed emotions. I felt a rush of fear, sorrow, rage, and then it all melted into total confusion.

Sensing that something wasn't right and fearing that I may have been in some kind of danger, Al broke the circle and I slumped to the floor exhausted and unsure of what had just happened. When I later related my experience to the others, one person said that he believed I had indeed made contact with the spirit of the insane woman who had been imprisoned in that room so very long ago. I had apparently been tapping into her thoughts and emotions, and experiencing the pain and confusion of her insanity.

We put out the candle, turned on the flashlight, and then proceeded to make our way down from the attic. Just as we reached the middle of the attic stairs, the spot where Marlene had first been overcome by emotion, 13 old square-headed nails materialized out of thin air and began to rain down upon us. Craig picked up a few of them and, after close examination, said he believed they were nails from a coffin.

It was about a year or so later when Al and I discovered an old wooded crucifix with the hand-carved figure of Jesus Christ nailed upon it hidden underneath one of the loose floorboards in the attic. We brought it downstairs to show my mother, who urged us to return it to the spot in which we found it. She said someone long ago had evidently put it there for a reason, perhaps to bring peace to the spirit in the attic, or maybe to drive away something evil. Whatever the reason, we returned the crucifix to its resting place beneath the attic floorboard.

A few weeks later, a friend of ours—a Native American woman from the nearby Mohawk Indian Reservation—came over with her young teenage daughter to visit. We had mentioned our finding of the crucifix in the attic and they were very curious to have a look at it and see what sort of psychic impressions they might receive from it. But when we took them upstairs and lifted up the floorboard to show it to them, the crucifix was not there. It had mysteriously vanished and was never to be seen again.

In the year and a half following its establishment, Coven Mandragora found itself faced with many trials and tribulations, including the tragic suicide of one of its members (which many folks, including myself, believe was actually a covered-up homicide). Irreconcilable differences and internal power struggles began to take precedence over our quest for spiritual enlightenment and the magickal arts, eventually laying the groundwork for the coven's demise. At the same time, a nosy neighbor who had spied on one or more of our outdoor sabbat rituals held around a blazing bonfire pit behind the house began spreading gossip to others in town that we were worshippers of the Devil and performed animal sacrifices at our bonfires—neither of which are even in the slightest bit true. However, the malicious rumors, and the fear and hatred they generated, were not to remain confined to the small town of Fort Covington for very long. We soon learned that people we did not even know were talking about our supposed "Satanic rituals" in places as far away as Massena, which is in another county!

I was becoming increasingly concerned that it was just a matter of time before some group of pious vigilantes tried to burn down our house (with us in it), in the holy name of their God and to save their innocent children from the evil that so many of them were convinced we were unleashing upon their backwoods, predominantly Christian community.

The final blow came when the devastating "icestorm of the century" hit the area in January of 1998, leaving portions of upstate New York and Canada without electricity and phone service for weeks. I nearly froze to death in my own home. The house sustained a great amount of damage, which was only partially covered by insurance, and nearly all of the once-beautiful trees that filled our yard either snapped like twigs or literally split in half from the weight of the accumulated ice. Power lines and poles were down everywhere, the roads were impassable, reports of people freezing to death in their homes or dying from carbon monoxide poisoning from indoor kerosene heaters were coming in over the radio daily, and a state of martial law had been declared. The entire area looked, and felt like, a bleak and frozen, war-torn battle zone.

I began to view all of this as a sign from the gods that my time to leave Fort Covington had arrived. As much as it saddened me to say farewell to my beloved Victorian on the hill and to the few former coven members with whom I remained close friends, we put the house up for sale and eventually left the area, returning once again to the sunny climes of Southern California.

Things That Go Bump in the Night

by Lee Prosser

I have a gift, but this gift is not for hire, and it is not for rent, but only for me to share with others in an effort to encourage them to develop this particular type of gift if they wish. For it is a wonderful gift and, like some wonderful gifts, it does not always work. When it does work, it opens the doors to interesting encounters. I can sense the presence of apparitions, or ghosts, as modern paranormal researchers define them. Sometimes I can visit with them, sometimes not.

My first awareness of this gift was when I was a child of six years. I was at my Grandmother Firestone's sister's Victorian house in Springfield, Missouri. Due to my inquisitive nature, I had managed to wander into an unused section of the rambling old house. I had followed a set of stairs to a small room with an open door, and inside was an antique toilet with the pull chain. Leaning up against the wall staring at me was an old man with a handlebar mustache. I said hello. He said hello. I said good-bye and walked back out of the room and continued my exploration of the house. Later, I told my Uncle Willard about what had happened and he said he knew that man and that he was a soul visiting the house. He explained it in this manner: "There are two worlds. The one in which you live; and the other, in which you do not but you can talk with. It is like seeing a rabbit go into its rabbit hole and linger, and you hear it and know it is there but it remains unseen until it is ready to show itself to you again. Nothing that comes to you is ever lost, and the memory of that visit may change with time, but that it came to you is what is important. Remember that when you encounter such things. Often, such things happen to teach you something or show you a secret. I have seen ghosts, and other things, too. It is nothing to be afraid of. Enjoy the meetings. Learn from them." From that point forward, I accepted the fact that there did exist ghosts and an attempt should be made to be friendly and peaceful when I came into contact with them.

I recall the three Native American ghosts on my Grandmother Firestone's land. Settled in the early 1850s by a German farmer named Rolf, there had at one time been a cabin at the back end of the property, off to the right. To this day, one can still see the wagon wheel indentations that led up to the cabin. Near where this cabin once stood, I saw an older Native American male, a younger Native American male, and a younger Native American woman. They had dark hair, and perhaps the older male was the father. The Indian woman with bright eyes waved to me and I waved back. Then, all three motioned to me, and I walked towards them. They were pointing to the ground. They smiled and vanished when I nearly reached them. I saw nothing on the ground. Perhaps it was something under ground they wanted me to see.

89

In every encounter I have ever had, there is a sense of the presence of something before I see it if I am allowed to see it, a pleasant tingling sensation that starts in my forehead where the Third Eye is located, and which spreads out across my skin. My skin tingles until the contact is broken and the ghost is gone away. I have often wondered if in the many theories surrounding the dead and ghosts, they in turn see the living as a ghostly apparition—a touching of one dimension upon another dimension. And who is the more real: the living person perceiving the dead, or the dead person perceiving the living? Does it matter? No. What matters is the contact established.

In Missouri I saw a black man sitting under a bridge fishing and he waved to me. I waved back. The group I was with asked who I was waving to and I told them. Everyone laughed, thinking I was making a joke when it was clear to them that nobody was visible under the bridge. I know what I saw. Another Missouri incident involved exploring the ruins of a two-story Victorian house and encountering the ghost of a woman in a long red dress who walked down a set of broken stairs and vanished in front of me, as if a door had opened and she had stepped into it.

When I lived in Salem, Oregon, I occupied a room with a view on the top floor of a three-story Victorian house. It was there that I encountered a young blond-headed man dressed in a 1930s era blue suit at the head of the stairs leading to my rented room. This took place twice. Each time I asked him if he was looking for somebody. He smiled, nodded yes, and went back down the steps. The second time this happened I followed him and watched him step off the steps as if to embrace a loved one and vanish. I discreetly asked around, and was told by an older tenant on the ground level that the couple that had once owned the house had a son killed in World War II, but did not know what had become of the former house owners. I never saw the young man again.

In Brodie, California, a preserved ghost town in the mountains, I saw a young woman with red hair, and she was wearing a white gingham dress. She was pretty, but sad and lonely. She was in one of the buildings that had caskets. I became aware of her at the same time she became aware of me. I wanted to touch her, but knew I could not. There was something wonderfully sensual about her. She sensed my curiosity about her as a person, and reached out her long fingers to me and smiled. I smiled back, hesitated. I took a photograph of her smiling. She beckoned to me, wanting to show me something. But I was not sure what it was she wanted. The people I was with joined me, then I walked on and she followed me for a while before returning to the building site, walking through the wall and vanishing. Much later, when the photographs were developed, the photo was perfect, but she was not in it, only the building and the caskets. I sometimes think it would be nice to return to this old ghost town and find out what she wanted to share with me.

Walking along the sidewalk in Santa Monica Canyon, California, during 1969, an old man approached me, walked through the couple walking behind me, and vanished. It was the first time I had ever had that happen and it was a weird feeling. The old man never gave any sign that he saw me or the couple walking behind me. I asked the couple if they felt anything just then and they said they felt an electrical current, which was the same thing I had felt. I walked on, curious as to what other secrets Santa Monica Canyon might hold in store for me. I encountered the ghost of a tall older woman walking the beach at Santa Monica but she walked into the ocean and vanished. She had the saddest smile.

91

When my grandmother Archie T. Firestone died in Missouri at 3:27 a.m. on October 31, 1971, she was beside me within moments even though I was living in California at the time. Like astral traveling, a dead person can be where he or she wishes to be instantly. We visited. When my Uncle Willard Firestone died on August 28, 1979, he was with me within a day. We visited. It was enjoyable being with them.

Once, while standing on the street in Lincoln, New Mexico, I saw two cowboys riding horses approaching me. They went past me and then vanished 10 feet away, but not before one of them—a big man in a brown coat and brown hat—turned and tipped his hat to me with a smile and a nod. I have an enduring affection for this little town that was the hangout of outlaw Billy the Kid. I am sure the ghosts of yesterday walk and ride through Lincoln, New Mexico, both daily and nightly.

I now live in the Southwest. At the end of my house, near the study where I write and paint, a small strawberry-blonde headed girl, approximately 10 years old and dressed in a flowing Edwardian summer dress of pink with white lace, comes and smiles at me. When I've see her standing there, I've tried to move towards her to make contact with her, but she always smiles, waves, and is gone. I hope another time to make that contact and understand why she is there. She is a lovely child ghost, and pleasant.

These are some of my remembrances of things past concerning ghosts. There have been other encounters, each time a different situation, but always friendly. I think every person has this gift that I have, either it is asleep and unused, or else it is full-blown and in full use. Being in contact with the dead and ghosts is as old as time. My gift is sometimes there, and sometimes it is not. But I am grateful for those abilities of the gift I was blessed with.

92

Sometimes I sense a presence and see nothing. Other times, I encounter that presence.

Not all things that go bump in the night are meant to alarm, most of them are meant to educate or share a moment in time with. Give it a try. It is an adventure available to all if people would only wake up to what is around them. We are never alone.

[Born under the sign of Capricorn, Lee Prosser is a researcher and legally recognized Interfaith minister who has held a lifelong interest in Wicca, Vedanta, and Shamanism. His published works include: *Running from the Hunter; Desert Woman Visions: 100 Poems; Isherwood, Bowles, Vedanta, Wicca and Me*; and *Night Tigers*. He resides in Oklahoma with his wife and their cats.]

The Lady in White

By Karri Ann Allrich

When I was going through a thorny period in my days of early motherhood, I had an experience with a female ghost that was at first unnerving, but eventually developed into a concerned, even comforting awareness. My marriage was in trouble. I had two small sons, and devoted my energy and effort to taking care of them; protecting them from the conflicts and struggles with their father.

One midsummer night as I lay sleeping, I was

stirred awake by a rising sense of unease. At first I suspected mother's instinct, and inclined one ear toward the open bedroom door, listening for the children. There was no sound. My husband was sound asleep next to me, oblivious. I waited in the dark, hearing nothing. Still I felt uneasy. I turned over on my back and listened harder. Suddenly I began to feel my skin prickle, as if I was being observed. I sat upright in bed and looked toward the bedroom door. There she was—a woman, silently watching me. Her appearance was filmy, not solid. There was no flesh and blood. This was a separate reality, a spirit from another world. A ghost. The moment I sat up and caught her image, she turned and vanished. Her quick departure held a certain shyness about it, as if she were embarrassed that she had been detected!

I was astounded, and no longer sleepy. I thought about her for the rest of the night, and I could not imagine why she was lingering in my bedroom. Our house was 50 years old, hardly antique. And no one had died in it. I mentioned the encounter to no one—especially not to the boys.

It was two weeks later when she appeared again. I was lying in the dark, restless with a foreboding sense of doom about my marriage, when I sensed her presence. This time when I glanced in her direction, she lingered for a moment before disappearing. I had the definite intuition that she was trying to tell me something. Over the course of that fitful summer, I would catch glimpses of her out of the corner of my eye, even during daylight. She seemed to linger in the bedroom, or the hallway just outside the bedroom door. I was no longer unnerved by her presence, just mildly curious. I never told anyone about her.

One rainy afternoon my older son was sitting on the family room floor amidst the usual tumble of construction paper, books and toys, drawing pictures with colored markers.

94

I was walking down the hall, coming from my bedroom. He looked up at me, then back down at his project before asking, quite casually, "Mom, who's that lady behind you?" I stood very still, astonished. He had seen her too! "What lady?" I asked.

"The lady in the white dress. I've seen her before."

I sat down with my son and told him, "She is a guardian spirit, perhaps an angel. She is watching over us. Are you afraid of her?"

"Not really," he answered.

By the end of the summer, my husband was gone, at my request. There was a sense of peace in the house. I had discovered that he had betrayed me, not once, but with several women. After his departure, I never saw the woman in white again. Looking back, I believe she had tried to warn me about the infidelity. I may never know her true connection to me, or why she appeared only to my first-born son and me, but I will always be grateful. Her spirit was gentle, and her presence comforting. She reminded me that we are never alone, even through terrible times.

[Karri Ann Allrich is an artist and the author of *A Witch's Book of Dreams; Cooking By Moonlight;* and *Recipes from a Vegetarian Goddess*. She shares her Massachusetts home and studio with her soulmate and husband Steve Allrich, also an artist and author. You may visit her on the Web at: *www.karriannallrich.cjb.net*]

The House in San Bernardino

By Tamara Thorne

Late in the 70s, we moved into a four-bedroom home, a typical tract house in an established, pleasant neighborhood in the north end of San Bernardino, California. The house 'felt' fine to me, but almost immediately weird little things began happening. Everything about the house felt fine, but within a few weeks of moving in, I saw a toothbrush pop out of the holder by the medicine cabinet, slipping straight up then tumbling into the sink. I thought it was simply interesting whenever it reoccurred, or when magazines would flop up over the edge of the basket I kept them in, or the Kleenex box slid across a nightstand and another foot beyond before dropping to the floor.

These things happened regularly, and I chalked them up to some kind of gravitational glitch because they didn't frighten me. That was the strange part. All my life I'd jumped at every noise and seen ghosts in every shadow. I couldn't watch or even listen to a scary movie without bolting. I always had a reputation for being the family scaredy cat. But here, in this houseful of phenomena, I was fine. There was no emotional sensation, so I knew it wasn't anything spooky.

Because it honestly seemed unimportant and because I didn't want to talk about something that could bring on the old teasing, I didn't tell anyone, even my husband. He wouldn't have teased though, and I think part of me knew that if I drew his attention to it, my blasé feelings might evolve into something unnerving.

For six months, these phenomena continued on a regular basis, minor and harmless. Then one Saturday we sat down for lunch at the kitchen table. We were side by side, facing into the room and a full trash box, about three and a half feet tall, was waiting in the center of the room to be taken out after we ate. We were both holding ham sandwiches on wheat and tall glasses of milk were in front of us. We were talking, joking around. And we were both looking forward when the trash box lifted off the floor. It levitated about two or three inches off the ground and hovered for several seconds. Then it dropped and sat there like nothing had happened.

We looked at each other and simultaneously said, "Did you see that?" We agreed we did and then I said, "It's just gravity," and explained that while I'd never seen anything so impressive before, that little things hopped around all the time. My mate was fascinated and spooked and used the "p" word—poltergeist. Despite my life-long fear, or because of it, I was well versed in paranormal phenomena and I guess my subconscious had kept that word out of my mind. Scary word!

Sure enough, in the next couple weeks, though nothing but the usual little phenomena occurred, the house began to feel menacing. I turned on all the lights as I moved down the halls and jumped at noises. Shadows seemed menacing now. I was most afraid that I'd buckle under the pressure and announce that we had to move. I would have before long, but the owners announced they wanted to move back in. What a relief!

The House in Tujunga

By Tamara Thorne

Tujunga, California, sits in the foothills a few miles above Los Angeles. It, like several other cities and towns along the edges of the Angeles and San Bernardino National Forests, has an odd feel to it. There's a loneliness and uneasiness to the area, faint, but there nonetheless. During the 80s, we rented a roomy single-story house there. It was a ranch house built in the 60s, nice but unremarkable. The sunny living room, dining room, and kitchen formed a circle at one end and beyond the front door at the edge of the living room, a dark hall contained four bedrooms and one bath. Our bedroom was at the far end. The floors were oak under carpet.

We lived there for six months and nothing overt occurred, but we were always uneasy there. Our five cats suddenly became clingy and insisted on sleeping with us. They'd never been interested before, but now they clawed the door if we shut them out. The only other thing that was strange (in retrospect) was the muscle twitch that began in my right shoulder. At night, when I'd go in the bathroom to brush my teeth, I'd feel a little tap, like someone touching my shoulder blade. It would happen most every night, just once, and had a slight electric feel to it. I wasn't concerned and never thought about it until it stopped after we moved out.

The night before we moved out, we had left our toddler with his grandmother and our cats at our new home then returned to the packed-up house to sleep on the mattress we'd left on the floor. In the morning, my spouse got up first, to go down to L.A. to borrow a truck from his company. I lazed in bed after he said goodbye. I heard him walk down the long hall and open and close the door.

A minute or two passed and I heard the front door open and close again. I thought he'd forgotten his wallet and called his name as I got up to find it. There was no reply, but I heard his footsteps coming slowly up the hall. They were heavier sounding than they should be and why was he walking so slowly? I called out again, yet there was no reply.

Adrenaline-charged now, half-sure I had a prowler, I pulled on a T-shirt and jeans and grabbed the only thing left in the room that could serve as a weapon—a broom. I held the handle in both hands, ready to poke a belly or bash a head, I moved behind the closed bedroom door and waited. A split second more and the footsteps stopped on the other side of the door. I announced I had a gun. No reply. Minutes passed. Finally, too charged up to stand there waiting any longer, I moved to the wall and slammed open the door, shoving the broom handle forward as fast as I could.

There was nothing there. I waited. And then heard footsteps again, down in the living room or kitchen. There was no window that would open easily. I had to go for the front door. My trusty broom-spear aimed forward, I stepped softly down the hall, trying not to creak the floor. I got to the end of the hall and paused, seeing no one. The footsteps stopped. The intruder was probably in the kitchen. I began to turn toward the front door, just a few feet out of the hall and, suddenly, the footsteps started up again, heavy and frightening, right behind me, trudging up the hall toward our bedroom.

I didn't look back—I just high-tailed it outside and waited for my mate. I had weathered the poltergeist phenomena years before in the house in San Bernardino, discounting it because it didn't affect my emotions. But this—I hate the word "evil" but that best describes the sensation I experienced. I wasn't positive there was a living prowler in the house anymore.

When my spouse arrived, he was more amused than worried. We went inside and stood in the foyer a moment looking around. As we stepped forward, the footsteps began in front of us and went a few yards up the hall and we heard the door to the first bedroom slam even though it didn't move. There was silence for a few moments, then the footsteps headed up the hall and faded away. With broom and crowbar in hand, we explored the house together, but there was nothing to see or hear.

Nothing happened again until late afternoon. We were almost done loading the truck and were flopped on the floor of the bedroom with the phantom door-slamming, drinking warm Cokes. My mate yelped suddenly and his lower leg jerked. He said something had yanked his ankle. I thought he was kidding. Still we finished up before dark and got out of there.

The next afternoon, he went back to give the key to the landlord, who hadn't yet arrived. My husband decided to take a last look through the house to make sure we hadn't left anything behind. He started in the garage and worked his way through the living areas and up the hall. He was in our bedroom when he heard the front door slam and footsteps head up the hall. He assumed it was the landlord and came out to greet him. There was no one there.

He locked up and left the key in the mailbox. Years later, I found out that a man who had lived there with his wife and child had gradually descended into a brain tumor-induced madness and regularly abused his family.

Paranormal research has revealed that hauntings activated by people moving out of a house are not uncommon. Perhaps our leaving set off the nasty footstep "tape" because the man's family left him.

[Tamara Thorne is a novelist specializing in the paranormal. Her books include *Haunted*, *Moonfall*, *Eternity*, *Candle Bay*, and *Bad Things*. Her newest novel, *The Forgotten*, is a ghost story, available as of November 2002. When not writing, Tamara spends much of her time researching hauntings and other phenomena both by book and in person.]

The Slumber Party Séance

By Sirona Knight

On my 11th birthday, I had a slumber party. Being born at Samhain, I always had parties with a Halloween theme. Six of my best friends and I stretched out our sleeping bags on the living room floor in front of our huge granite stone fireplace. The fire kept the room warm while we ate chocolate cake and ice cream and talked—about boys of course!

We talked for about two hours, finished the cake, and had started in on the potato chips. We put another log on the fire, and then turned off the lights. We all sat there watching the fire flames for a few minutes. There was mystery and intrigue in the air. I thought it would be fun to do a séance. There were seven willing participants, and after all, it was the night after Halloween. Everyone was totally into it, so we joined our hands together, séance style. The whole idea was to talk with a ghost. We just wanted to keep it simple, talk with someone that had passed over, to ask what it was like.

We sat together with our hands joined, eyes open, in the relative dark. The flames from the fireplace created a perfect backdrop to the experience. I suggested that we say something like, "Please spirit show yourself and talk with us." So we all kept repeating the words, "Spirit, show yourself and talk with us." We did this for about five minutes, and then a face suddenly appeared by the living room window—not outside of the window, but inside the window, in the room with us! Two friends and myself saw the face immediately and just gasped, held our breath, and tightened our grip on one another's hands.

It was just a face without a body, a man's face, from the neck up. It looked like a holograph, filled with white-yellow light, but in constant motion. The face itself reminded me of a statue of a Greek god. The man's face kept moving, opening and closing his mouth, as if he were trying to say something. He wasn't frightening, just unnerving. I could feel the hair on the back of my neck and all over my arms stand on end. It felt like I had put my finger into the proverbial light socket.

As soon as the others turned around to see the face, they started screaming, got up, and ran outside into the front yard. I told them to stop screaming because I didn't want my parents to get uptight. Besides, I was very curious about what had materialized. Where did it come from? Who was it? Did he want to tell us something? Was it something important? I had a lot of pressing questions for the face!

Everyone finally quieted down, but did not want to go back into the house. We sat outside for about 15 minutes, but it was too cold to stay out long, so we all went back inside.

We talked for a while about the face, and then watched television. As we fell asleep, the face appeared once more, and then disappeared again. No one was able to sleep very well that night, but I will always remember the slumber party séance on my 11th birthday. And I will always wonder about the face we all clearly saw on that crisp November night.

[Sirona Knight is a Third Degree Craftmaster and High Priestess of the Celtic Gwyddonic Druid Tradition. She is a contributing editor for *Magical Blend* magazine and the author of a number of books on Celtic spirituality, magick, and Wicca, including *Celtic Traditions*, *Dream Magic*, *The Pocket Guide to Crystals and Gemstones*, *The Wiccan Spell Kit*, and *A Witch Like Me*. Her Website is: *www.sironaknight.com*]

Chapter 3

Spiritualism

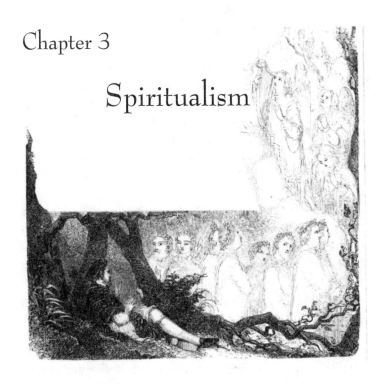

"At birth we are all given the gift of seeing beyond this humble Earth plane into other dimensions, but as we grow older we cast this natural ability aside. Mediums did not lose this ability and are people who act as intermediaries between this world and the 'other side.'"
—Larry Dreller, author of *Beginner's Guide to Mediumship*

The Early Years of Spiritualism

The spiritualism movement began in the United States in the mid-19th century. It rapidly gained popularity throughout both America and England. Appealing to a public made receptive by the earlier psychism-based movements (such as mesmerism) that originated in Europe and crossed the Atlantic to the United States.

Dr. William F. Williams, general editor of *Encyclopedia of Pseudoscience*, defines spiritualism as "a way of thinking that believes in immaterial reality, that is, knowledge perceived to be extrasensory that is by some means other than through the normal senses." He believes that "the great upsurge in the 19th century of belief in spiritualism" can be attributed to people's need to join together their spirituality with "their faith in the new materialism of science."

The original purpose of the spiritualism movement was to provide the world with evidence of life after the death of the physical body, which was manifested through spiritualist mediums gifted with the abilities to communicate with those in the hereafter and, in some cases, perform paranormal feats. But, by the late 1800s, an increasing number of fraudulent mediums came to be publicly exposed, seriously tarnishing the image of spiritualism, impairing the public's faith in mediums, and signaling the demise of spiritualism as a widespread cohesive movement. It later saw a resurgence of popularity both during and after the first World War, as great numbers of people turned to mediums in the hopes of making contact with husbands, sons, and brothers who gave their lives to serve their country.

Although it can be fair to say that spiritualism reached its peak in the early part of the 20th century, the movement continues to be a fascination for many in our modern times. It is kept alive in the 21st century by both mental and physical mediums, spiritual healers, and spiritualist churches, which continue to have followings in many parts of the world—including the United States, Brazil, and especially Great Britain, where there is said to exist spiritualist churches numbering well into the thousands!

> "From earliest beginnings man has used "natural" means to catch a glance beyond the curtain that hid the future and to get into contact with the supernatural. But in modern times he also devised artificial aids to help him in his endeavors. One of the more popular ones in spiritualist circles is the Ouija board." —R. Brasch. *Strange Customs*.

Communicating With Spirits Through a Ouija Board

The basic concept of the Ouija board is said to date back to Pythagoras in 540 BC, and it is known that Chinese diviners used devices for divination and communicating with the spirit world long before the birth of Confucius. According to Richard Webster's *Spirit Guides and Angels*, "The concept of the refined Ouija board was invented in 1853 by French spiritualist, M. Planchette" and utilized a heart-shaped wooden wedge mounted on casters and with an attached pencil, which, when one or more persons lightly rested their fingertips upon it, would be made to move over a large piece of paper, drawing "spirit pictures" and/or spelling out words.

An important tool of divination and a means to communicate with the spirits of the dead and other entities outside of our plane of existence, the modern Ouija board as we know it (with letters and numbers printed on it) was invented in the early 1890s by Elija J. Bond and William

Fund in Baltimore, Maryland, and introduced to the American public as a parlor game sold in novelty shops. Parker Brothers purchased all rights to the Ouija board in 1966 and, according to Richard Webster, its sales have been second only to the popular board game, Monopoly. Its name is said to be a fusion of the French word *oui* and the German word *ja*, both which mean "yes."

My first Ouija board was given to me as a birthday gift when I was around nine or 10 years of age, and since then I have always possessed one. Although I do not use it terribly often, I have made good use of it in the channeling of spirits, the finding of lost objects, and divination of the future. I have also used it, rather successfully, in conjunction with a crystal dowsing-pendulum that I purchased at a unique souvenir shop on a Mohawk Indian Reservation in upstate New York.

Although a Ouija board can be used by one person alone, better results are usually obtained when two people (preferably a male and a female) operate the board together. The couple should be seated in comfortable chairs and facing each other with the board resting on their laps. They should place fingertips very lightly on the message indicator and ask out loud one question at a time. It is important that both persons concentrate deeply while working with the board and not give in to impatience. Results are not always immediate. The amount of time it takes to establish contact with the spirit world depends greatly upon each individual's level of psychic ability and receptiveness, as well as upon a particular spirit's willingness or ability to communicate with the living. Working with a Ouija board made of solid wood is said to improve reception.

It is often beneficial to have an additional person (not working the board) in attendance to transcribe the entire session in case the planchette (also known as the indicator or pointer) begins moving too quickly for you to read and process the words that are being spelled out. Transcription is also helpful if a spirit message is received in reverse, scrambled, or in the form of an anagram, which is not at all uncommon. Another way to transcribe a Ouija board session is for one person to call out the letters and numbers into a nearby tape recorder as they are being indicated.

Be warned, however, that spirits are notorious for providing false or incorrect information. Many spirits contacted through a Ouija board are nothing more than pranksters, some of which take great delight in masquerading as historical figures, sages, and great teachers. Others are malicious liars with the intent to confuse those gullible enough to take everything they say as the undisputed truth.

In *Communing with the Spirits*, author Martin Coleman advises necromancers using a Ouija board to, "never be impressed by the supposed credentials of any spirits, and to never accept the words of any spirit at face value." He suggests that you question a spirit very carefully, never asking it any question to which you already know the answer, in case the spirit is able to read your thoughts. Instead, "you must always ask the spirit questions to which you can learn the answer."

Skeptics of the occult arts believe that the answers spelled out on a Ouija board are not created by the spirit world or any other paranormal forces, but rather by the conscious or unconscious mind of the person or persons using the board.

One simple way to determine whether or not actual contact with the dead has been made is to let those operating the board be blindfolded while a third party observes and records on paper what letters and/or numbers are selected.

If the results add up to gibberish, then chances are that no contact was made. However, keep in mind that spirits are known to sometimes speak in riddles, ancient languages (such as Latin, Greek, or Arabic), or spell out their answers in an anagrammatic fashion (with letters transposed to form a new word or phrase). So be sure to carefully analyze all messages that come through the Ouija board, regardless how unintelligible they may initially appear.

I have also heard numerous opponents of the Ouija board frantically warn others against using it on the grounds that it is a "dangerous toy" (as they often refer to it) that will ultimately lead to the demonic possession of those who use it to summon and communicate with spirits. Interestingly, I have found nearly all of these crusaders who preach such nonsense to either be occult-fearing Christians or those of the Christian-turned-Pagan sect, who, behind their quasi-New Age exteriors, still retain many or all of the Christian beliefs, fears, and hang-ups that were instilled in them at an early age by the Church— one of them being the Christian idea that it is a sin to conjure or converse with the spirits of the dead. With my personal views on Christianity and religion aside, I can honestly say that I have never experienced any "demonic" problems by using a Ouija board or having one in my house, nor do I personally know of any well-grounded Witches or occultists who have.

I strongly suspect that in addition to such Christian-based fears, one of the reasons many individuals—young persons in particular—find the Ouija board to be such a fearful thing is because of the vast number of fictional horror films that have portrayed it as being a sinister tool or toy, depending on how you wish to look at it, capable of unleashing untold demonic horrors upon the unsuspecting mortal world. However, it is important to bear in mind that the keyword here is *fictional* and to be aware that movies are just that. The occult and those who practice it have seldom, if ever, been portrayed very accurately in movies (or in most plays, novels, and television shows for that matter). All one needs to do is take a look at how the motion picture industry has been instrumental in perpetuating the negative stereotyping of Witches and other Pagans over the last century, and that should settle my case once and for all!

This is not to say that the Ouija board cannot create an open door to the spirit world through which a malevolent earthbound spirit or other uninvited entity can come. It very well can, unless the board is used in a safe and proper manner, and the person operating it is in a healthy state of mind. (Note: Those who have a history of mental illness should, under no circumstances, ever operate a Ouija board! Interaction with a malicious spirit can be very psychologically damaging to certain individuals.) By observing certain simple precautions (which are outlined below), the chances of any harm coming from it are slim to none. Under these conditions, there is no real reason to fear the Ouija board. It is no more, or no less, dangerous than holding a séance or performing any other ritual or divination that makes contact with the spirit world.

Precautionary Measures:

1. Always create a clockwise circle around you and the Ouija board before attempting to make contact with spirits. The circle, which provides protection against harmful spirits, can either be drawn on the ground using chalk or a trail of salt, or drawn invisibly in the air with the blade of a consecrated athame (a double-edged ritual dagger). A circle of

candles is also effective for creating a safe and protected space in which to work, while holding a session in a well-lit area is believed by some to keep evil spirits at bay (who are said to prefer darkness over light).

2. Take care never to leave or uncast the circle until after you have said good-bye to whatever spirit you have evoked, thus ending the session and severing the link of communication between the spirit and you. Some spiritualists believe that if the spirit fails to reply in kind, this may be an indication that the spirit is unwilling to leave. The best thing to do in such a case is to command the spirit to leave at once and in peace. If this fails to do the trick, the next step is for you to pray to your God or Goddess to make the spirit permanently leave your home. After doing this, proceed to fumigate every room in your house with an incense made of equal parts by weight of cardamom and ginger or of frankincense and thyme.

3. Silver is a metal that has long been regarded as possessing the power to repel and protect against all manners of evil. Many spiritualists, therefore, use a silver coin in place of the planchette and/or wear a silver pentagram or some other type of silver jewelry during Ouija board sessions. I always wear a silver ring bearing the symbol of a black pentagram on my ring finger whenever engaging in divinations and magickal workings.

4. It is recommended that a Ouija board be used no more than a few hours each week.

If a person feels compelled to use it more often, this could be a warning sign of obsession. And, as a rule, young children should not be allowed to use, or play with, a Ouija aboard as they tend to be considerably more impressionable than adults, which makes the risk of obsession all the greater for them.

5. Anyone under the influence of alcohol or drugs should refrain from working with a Ouija board. The same goes for those who are in an unhealthy emotional or mental state, as contact with spirits of a negative nature can sometimes lead them to depression, an unhealthy obsession with death, and thoughts of suicide.

6. Lastly, and perhaps most importantly, I would strongly urge you to immediately bring your Ouija board session to a close and put the board away if you should suddenly begin to feel threatened in any way by a spirit.

Séances, and How to Conduct Them

"The séance, or sitting, offers the opportunity to establish a bridge and a relationship with the departed spirits in another sphere."
—Anna Riva

Also known in modern times as a "sitting" or a "spirit-circle," a séance (the French word for "sitting") is the gathering of a given number of persons for the purpose of seeking communication with the spirits of persons recently deceased or of those who have been long dead. It is said that the traditional séance as we know it was invented by the Fox sisters in the mid-19th century, although the practice of communicating with the dead is probably as old as

111

mankind itself. Leah Fox, who began her career in spiritualism in the year 1849, is believed to be the world's first professional medium.

Séances can be held either at night or during the daytime hours, but are more effective when held in a darkened room illuminated by the glow of a burning candle or small oil lamp, which is usually placed on the center of the table where those attending the séance will sit. It is said that strong light produces excessive motion in the atmosphere, which is disturbing to the manifestations. A round or oval table is preferred, and the room should be well ventilated and free of minerals and glass objects, as their energies have been known to interfere with reception in some psychic-sensitive individuals. Conduct a séance at a time when it will not be interrupted, and be sure to unplug the phone and turn off all radios and televisions. The more quiet, the better. In order for a séance to serve its purpose, it is also imperative that all persons present have an open and positive mind so that phenomena may occur.

Ideally, the number of persons in attendance of a séance should be three at minimum and twelve at maximum. According to some sources, the number of participants must be divisible by the number three. At least one medium (a person through whom the spirits speak and act) must be present. However, no more than two well-developed mediums should ever attend the same séance. Persons in poor health, and especially those with weak hearts, should avoid attending, unless the sitting is assembled expressly for healing purposes. In addition, it is not recommended that young children, persons suffering from mental disorders or depression, individuals possessing an extremely skeptical or negative attitude towards the séance, anyone under the influence of alcohol or drugs, and any person not psychologically equipped to handle communicating with the dead, attend a séance.

Some mediums work with the aid of a control. Also referred to as a "spirit helper" by many modern mediums, a control is a spirit that a medium makes contact with after entering an altered state of consciousness during a séance. The control either communicates mentally with the medium or speaks directly through his or her vocal chords to convey messages from other spirits to the persons seated at the séance table.

Before a séance commences, it is helpful to have a tape recorder nearby to record it, or an observer with notepad and pencil in hand to make note of any paranormal phenomena that might manifest during the séance and to copy down any spirit messages that may come through the medium.

Everyone, including the medium, should be seated comfortably around the table. They should relax, close their eyes, and visualize for a minute or so being surrounded by a white spiraling light. Many Witches who hold séances cast an invisible clockwise circle of protection around the séance area with a consecrated athame. Next, all persons should form a living circle by joining hands—left hand up and right hand down to complete the circuit. This circle should not be broken at any time during the course of the séance, unless necessity or indisposition should warrant it. Breaking the circle while a séance is in progress will not only sever the line of communication between the spirit world and the living, in some instances it can also cause trauma to the medium if he or she should happen to be in a deep trance at that moment. (Some modern spiritualists feel that the holding or touching of hands during a séance is unnecessary. As long as all hands are laid upon the table with palms downwards, the wood of the table, when charged, acts as a conductor of spiritual energy.)

Many séances are opened with a special chant or a prayer, sometimes the recitation of Psalm 23, which is as follows: "The Lord is my shepherd; I shall not want. He maketh me to lie down in green pastures: he leadeth me beside the still waters. He restoreth my soul: he leadeth me in the paths of righteousness for his name's sake. Yea, though I walk through the valley of the shadow of death, I will fear no evil: for thou art with me; thy rod and thy staff they comfort me. Thou preparest a table before me in the presence of mine enemies: thou anointest my head with oil; my cup runneth over. Surely goodness and mercy shall follow me all the days of my life: and I will dwell in the house of the Lord forever." (King James version.)

A prayer more appropriate for Pagans gathered for a séance would be as follows:

> *"O Lady and Lord of love and of light,*
> *O ancient ones of darkness and might,*
> *Empower this circle by all of your charms,*
> *Shield us from evil; protect us from harm.*
> *Grant us ascendancy, thrice by Thee blessed,*
> *to make the spirits manifest.*
> *Many thanks we give to Thee,*
> *This is our will; so mote it be!"*

It is important that all participants concentrate upon the individual whose spirit they seek to contact. A photograph and/or personal effects once belonging to the deceased person may be placed on the table to aid concentration and to send out energy vibrations, which the spirit will hopefully receive and respond to. The séance begins when its conductor (often the medium) calls out to the spirit world in an effort to make contact with those who have crossed over to "the other side" (as the spirit world has come to be known). Typically, something along the following lines will be spoken:

> "We are gathered in this circle in the hopes of making contact with the world beyond that of the living. In that world there is one we wish to communicate with. One who was known in life as [name]. If this spirit can hear us and is willing to speak, please come forth to us from beyond the darkness and silence of the grave, and give us a sign."

After calling out to the spirit, be patient and wait for a response. If none is received within a reasonable amount of time, continue calling to the spirit until it responds, or try contacting a different one that might be more receptive and give you a sign.

Often, the sign of a spirit's presence will come in the form of a rapping or other sound audible to all, a sudden cold chill, or the sensation of a passing breeze. Sometimes the flame of the candle will react by turning blue and/or flickering rapidly or burning unusually high. In some cases, a spirit will speak in a disembodied voice, visibly manifest, or cause the table to levitate or objects (known as apports) to materialize out of thin air.

After receiving the spirit's sign, proceed to ask it whatever questions you may have for it. Ask only one yes-or-no question at a time, and instruct the spirit to answer you by rapping once for yes and twice for no (or vice versa if you prefer) or to use the medium as an instrument through which to speak.

No two séances are ever identical to one another. Sometimes it can take a great while before contact with a spirit can be established, and other times it can be almost instantaneous. In some cases, a spirit is unable or unwilling to communicate with the living and no contact at all will be made. A failure to make contact with the spirit world can also result if the level of concentration is weak, if the medium's health or energy is not up to par, or if the séance is continually interrupted by distractions such as a ringing telephone, the barking of a dog, a crying baby, traffic noises,or the like.

In less common instances, a person who had never before displayed any psychic or mediumistic abilities will suddenly fall into a trance during the course of a séance and have a spirit speak through them. Rarely do these types of experiences ever pose any threat of danger, and the person normally retains little or no recollection of the experience after returning from the trance to a full state of consciousness. Such an experience may indicate the awakening of one's natural gift of mediumship, or it may be a one-time occurrence never to be repeated.

If, during the séance, one should suddenly feel the urge to speak, sing, gesticulate, or write, he or she should not try to suppress it, as it may be a spirit's way of expressing itself through that individual. Should a dark and evil spirit happen to be encountered, it should not be driven away. Instead, all should strive to elevate it and treat it as they would a living person in similar circumstances.

It is important that control is maintained during a séance. If it is felt that the situation is starting to get out of hand (participants are becoming upset, the medium appears to have lost control, etc.), it is perfectly acceptable under such conditions that the séance be brought to an immediate halt. This is accomplished simply by breaking the circle of hands, putting out the candle, and switching on the light.

A séance should always last for a minimum of one hour (even if no contact with the spirit world is made) and no more than two hours unless the spirit solicits an extension in time. When all have finished communing with the spirit and are ready to bring the séance to a close, the conductor should be sure to give thanks to the spirit for joining the séance and politely instruct it to go forth in peace. The circle of hands should then be broken and the flame of the candle extinguished.

Chapter 4

The Necromantic Arts

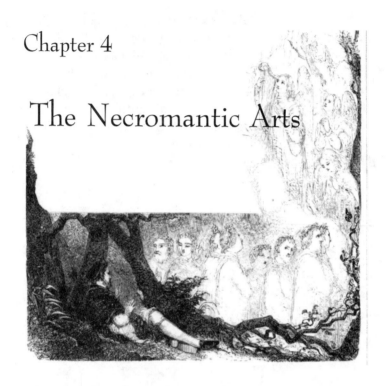

"Witchcraft, in its necromantic, thaumaturgic, and apotropaic diversity, has invariably been a significant phenomenon of all cultures, at whatever level of development."
—Harry E. Wedeck, *Treasury of Witchcraft*

Necromancy is the art and practice of divination by conjuring up, and communicating with, the spirits of the dead. In *The Women's Encyclopedia of Myths and Secrets*, Barbara Walker states that necromancy is "one of the world's most popular forms of magic, still widely practiced under the new name of spiritualism or mediumship."

Necromancy, from the Greek *nekros* (a dead body) and *manteia* (divination), is rooted in antiquity, like so many of the occult arts. It has been practiced throughout the world by numerous cultures, including the ancient Greeks, Romans, Celts, and Persians, who employed it as a means to learn the secrets of the after-life, as well as to unveil the future.

Webster's New Encyclopedia of Dictionaries defines necromancy as "black magic," and for centuries necromantic rites have been called "the black arts." However, contrary to popular misconception, necromancy is not necessarily a form of black magick, nor does it involve the conjuring of demons or the Devil. According to J.B. Russell in *Witchcraft in the Middle Ages*, necromancy came to be known as "the black arts" after the Greek root *nekros* was corrupted to Latin *niger*, meaning "black." Thus, nigromancy (another word for necromancy) loosely translates to the "black method of divination" and is sometimes misused to indicate black magick.

Francis Barrett, author of the 19th century grimoire, *The Magus*, said the art of necromancy "has its name because it works on the bodies of the dead, and gives answers by the ghosts and apparitions of the dead, and subterraneous spirits, alluring them into the carcasses of the dead by certain hellish charms and infernal invocations, and by deadly sacrifices and wicked oblations."

One of the earliest written accounts of necromancy can be found in the Old Testament. Described as a "woman that hath a familiar spirit," the infamous Witch of Endor evokes the spirit of the dead Hebrew prophet Samuel in order to answer King Saul's questions. However, the conjured apparition foretells the king's doom.

Apollonius of Tyana was a Greek philosopher, prophet, and necromancer of the first century. Called "one of the most extraordinary persons that ever appeared in the world" by Francis Barrett, Apollonius was said to have been gifted with great supernatural powers. He was skilled in the arts of magick and reputed to possess the ability to communicate with birds. After falling out of favor with Emperor Severus, Apollonius was put on trial and ordered to have his hair sheared off in an effort to render his magickal abilities impotent.

In the 19th century, magician and author Eliphas Levi used a necromantic ritual to conjure the spirit of Apollonius of Tyana. In his book, *The Mysteries of Magic* (also known as *The Histories of Magic*), Levi wrote, "Three times and with closed eyes I invoked Apollonius. When again I looked forth there was a man in front of me, wrapped from head to foot in a species of shroud...he was lean, melancholy and beardless." The spirit, which Levi never acknowledged as actually being Apollonius, vanished after he commanded it to depart, using a ritual sword. However, it later reappeared before him. In the words of Levi, "The apparition did not speak to me, but it seemed that the questions I had designed to ask, answered themselves in my mind."

Necromancy is often associated with Pagans, particularly sorcerers and Witches. However, many Christians and Jews also believed in, and practiced, necromantic rites. Saint Clement the Roman was said to have hired a necromancer to conjure a spirit from the underworld and acquire from it the secrets of the after-life. Even Jesus Christ, on whose teachings the religious tradition of Christianity was founded, took on the role of a necromancer. In despite of this, the Catholic Church condemned necromancy as "the agency of evil spirits." According the Barbara Walker, "Christian authorities reserved for themselves all dealings with the dead and regarded any lay necromantic or spiritualist activities as heresy, if not diabolism."

In Elizabethan England, the practice of necromancy became a crime under the Witchcraft Act of 1604. In the year 1866, shortly after the birth of the spiritualist movement in

England and the United States, the Second Plenary Council of Baltimore forbade the faithful to hold or attend séances for any reason, ascribing a portion of spirit manifestations to "Satanic intervention since in no other manner can they be understood or explained."

After being officially banned by the Church, the practice of necromancy gained popularity (as do most things when they become "forbidden fruits"). However, its reputation tarnished as sorcerers began desecrating graves and exhuming the bodies of those who had recently died. According to author R. Brasch in *Strange Customs: How Did They Begin?*, "Murders were actually committed to use the corpse, in all its freshness, to reach the realm of the dead in order to gain from there a knowledge of the future."

Some necromancers were said to have even engaged in sexual intercourse with female corpses (necrophilia) for divinatory purposes. Such perversions were carried out in the belief that the life-giving potency of the necromancer's semen would revitalize the dead body and enable it to answer the call and supply the information that was requested.

"Through the ages a vast and exacting ritual was developed to summon the dead," says R. Brasch, "and it was applied by the sorcerers who became experts in necromancy." Magick circles, altars, tripods, bells, and magnetized iron became the tools of the trade for the necromancer, along with mystical incantations and the pentagram symbol (for protection).

An old necromantic ritual instructs the magician to wear upon his heart a Pentacle of Solomon and "approach the grave of the chosen corpse at sunset or midnight." After drawing a circle around the grave, a traditional (but highly poisonous) incense of mandrake, henbane, hemlock, saffron, opium, and wood aloe is burned in a censer. The lid of the coffin should then be opened. The magician "turns himself to all of the four winds," and then touches the corpse thrice with a wand held in his right hand, while firmly commanding the spirit of the deceased person to return to its former body and answer all questions put to it. [It is imperative that the corpse be arranged so that the top of its head points east and its arms and legs are "in the position of Christ when he was crucified."] After the magician's questions have been answered, the spirit is then made to depart and the corpse is burned.

Spirits are said to have access to information of the past and the future, which is unavailable to the living. Through necromantic rites, a magician is able to gain possession of such information. A spirit summoned by a necromancer can also be employed to locate buried or sunken treasure, and to reveal the cause of a person's death. According to *The Book of Black Magic and Ceremonial Magic*, "Moreover, it can answer very punctually concerning the places where ghosts reside, and the manner of communicating with them, teaching the nature of astral spirits and hellish beings, so far as its capacity alloweth."

Many necromancers are drawn to professions that deal with death and which allow them access to human cadavers. Since the digging up of graves in neither practical nor legal, practitioners of the necromantic arts can frequently be found working in such places as funeral homes, morgues, and cemeteries.

One of the most common misconceptions pertaining to necromancy is that all necromancers are Satanists or that their art is an offshoot of Satanism. While some necromancers might very well possess satanic views or even be card-carrying members of the Church of Satan, many others do not. Necromancy and Satanism are two very distinct paths. Necromancy, in itself, does not incorporate or advocate satanic worship, satanic evocations, satanic pacts, or sacrificial rites in the Devil's name. A belief in, or worship of, the Prince of Darkness is in no way requisite for becoming a necromancer. However, magickal skill and respect for the dead are.

While a common practice in the Voodoo religion, necromancy is seldom, if ever, practiced by Neo-Pagan Witches, many of whom regard it as evil, unethical, or serving no purpose. This is not to say that Witches cannot, or should not, practice the Black Art if they should feel it to be their calling.

Interview With a Necromancer

I recently had the opportunity to meet, and engage in an in-depth conversation with an individual who is not only very knowledgeable about the necromantic arts, but has practiced them for many years. The following questions and answers are the results from my interview with this fascinating individual, whose identity I have been asked to keep confidential.

Q: **Why have you chosen to practice necromancy?**

A: For the same reason that one practices any form of conjuration or sorcery...for *power*, to put it plain and simple! Power as a means to an end, and for whatever magickal goal I may have at the moment. As for others, some individuals become attuned to necromancy after the death of a loved one, while others are gifted with necromantic abilities at birth. For those of the latter group, necromancy is a part of who and what they are by nature.

Q: **Can necromancy be classified as a religious or spiritual path in addition to being a divinatory art?**

A: I define religion as a belief in, and reverence for, a supernatural power considered to be the creator, creatress, or controller of the universe. Therefore, I do not consider necromancy to be my religion...perhaps a *supplement* to my religion (which is Paganism). I view necromancy as being more of a school of thought. The ancient Druids studied the wisdom of the dead, as did the Babylonians, the priests of Osiris, and others throughout history. However, if a person is of the belief that necromancy is what controls the universe, then I suppose it could very well be classified as a religious or spiritual path for that particular individual. However, a lot of people would consider that to be nothing more than pure blasphemy! It is important to note that very few necromancers are necromancers for religious purposes. Most that I know, or have read about, practice it as a divinatory art, discipline, study, or class of magick.

Q: What do you feel are some of the reasons people are drawn to the practice of necromancy?

A: I think many practitioners are lured by the power that the necromantic arts can offer, and many find it to be a wholly rewarding and enlightening thing to do. There are, of course, those who are motivated by other reasons, such as the desire to communicate with a deceased loved one or simply out of curiosity to see if necromancy actually works.

Q: What are some of the myths and misconceptions associated with necromancy?

124

A: Many people assume necromancy is all about summoning the Devil or conjuring demons, which it isn't. Not all necromancers are Satanists, devil-worshippers, necrophiliacs, cannibals, or grave robbers. Many of us are decent, law-abiding individuals who raise families and maintain full-time employment or rewarding careers. Necromancers can be found in just about every community, but are extremely secretive about their art. For all you know, one might be living across the street or right next door to you.

Q: **Can necromancy be dangerous?**

A: There are undeniably many dangers associated with necromancy, and anyone who thinks otherwise (especially where high necromancy is concerned) is little more than a fool, or at least inclined to madness! The biggest danger facing the necromancer is his thinking that he has complete control over whatever spirit he has raised. As it is with any of the so-called "Black Arts," the necromancer is always at risk of succumbing to the very forces he is seeking to harness. That is why keeping concentration and mind set are of the utmost importance. It is important to remember that communicating with the dead is an extremely fragile thing. A practitioner of necromancy must always treat the dead with respect and know the right things to say. The threat of being astrally attacked by angry or curious entities is omnipresent. There are also side effects that come with the channeling of too much negative energy. Prolonged exposure to the powers of death can take a heavy toll upon a necromancer's body and mind, causing him to become more like the undead under his control. This corruption is typically a slow process that goes unnoticed for a long time as the necromancer, consumed by his studies, ignores or fails to recognize the initial effects. But eventually the strains imposed can eat away at one's physical, emotional, and mental well-being.

Q: **You mentioned "high necromancy." Can you elaborate on this?**

A: High necromancy is one of the most sacred and enigmatic of all necromantic rites. It is basically an invocation of Azrael, the Angel of Death, which enables the necromancer to align his soul with "death energy" (the current of transition). High necromancy permits a magician to share intimate consciousness with Azrael and to learn from that union. In high necromancy, an actual corpse is used as a catalyst.

Q: **What is the difference between so-called "black" necromancy and "white" necromancy?**

A: I have always considered black necromancy to basically be the summoning of an evil spirit or the raising of a dead body for the purpose of scaring, harming, or bringing death to another person, such as an enemy. It is an extremely dangerous thing to do and can quite easily backfire on the person trying to control the spirit. Black necromancy should only be performed by a master necromancer, if ever at all.

126

White necromancy, on the other hand, is the summoning of the dead for the purpose of divining the future or the unknown, or for the purpose of spiritual or magickal enlightenment. There are some, however, who simply define black necromancy as the raising of a corpse, and white necromancy as the summoning of a spirit.

Q: **Do you consider necromancy to be the best method of divination?**

A: I personally don't feel that there exists any one method of divination superior to all others. It all comes down to a matter of personal choice. What appeals to, or works well for one person might not necessarily for the next. Necromancy, like most occult practices, has its good points and its not-so-good points. And depending on the energies of the magician and the individual summoned, it can be either rewarding or unreliable. But one thing is for sure; it will never yield a dull experience! Necromancy can, without a doubt, be the most dangerous method of divination. But, on the other hand, it can also be the most powerful.

Q: **What are the best times and places to perform necromancy?**

A: Sunset or between the hours of midnight and 1 a.m. are the ideal times for summoning the spirits of the dead. Nights when the moon is full are good times as well. Traditionally, the places at which to perform necromancy have been graveyards (where spirits abound) and crossroads. Places such as these resonate with

127

strong magickal energies. However, necro-mantic rites can be performed in other loca-tions, such as a haunted dwelling, a sacred temple, or the spot where a death (either by natural or unnatural causes) occurred. Some necromancers have been known to work their magick in the dark of the desert or cloaked by the tangled trees of a forest.

Q: **What are some of the common mistakes made by novice necromancers?**

A: Many individuals try to perform necromancy thinking that they are in control of the dead, or that they can bring back the dead by their will alone or only with components and no spell. In all actuality, they haven't the slight-est idea what they're doing. There are always consequences that arise when one performs a necromantic rite, but some people fail to realize this. And that, in turn, can be a very dangerous thing. Attempting to raise the dead without the proper knowledge and training is a serious mistake, as not properly summon-ing, binding, dismissing, or banishing a spirit can greatly anger it. Know what you are do-ing before you try your hand at necromancy, otherwise you may very well put yourself, and those around you, in great danger!

Q: **What words of advice can you offer those interested in practicing necromancy?**

A: Necromancy should *never* be thought of as some kind of parlor game. It is serious busi-ness and is not intended for causing mischief or alleviating boredom. Additionally, raising the dead should never be attempted for the

128

purpose of carrying out evil deeds or bringing harm and misfortune to others, no matter what they might have done to you. This is a dangerous thing to do! (Especially for a neophyte.) Take care that you are well protected during necromantic rituals in case an evil spirit should materialize and try to do you harm. Wear a Pentacle of Solomon and always work within a circle, never stepping outside of it until after the spirit you summoned has been properly dismissed. I cannot stress this enough. There are cases of necromancers who conjured up an evil spirit but didn't know they had because the spirit was invisible. They foolishly stepped outside of the protective circle and were attacked. It is also a good idea to have an assistant with you in the circle whenever performing necromancy. Most masters of necromancy always work with an assistant. Study and train to become an adept magician before attempting necromancy. But keep in mind that knowledge without discipline can be a dangerous thing. In necromancy, it can get you, or those around you, killed!

Chapter 5
Possession, Obsession, and Exorcism

There are basically two types of possession: spirit and demonic. The first is described by Rosemary Ellen Guiley in her book, *The Encyclopedia of Witches and Witchcraft*, as "a voluntary culturally sanctioned displacement of personality," while the latter is said to be a complete takeover of an individual's personality by a demonic entity for the sole purpose of harm.

Spirit possession is practiced in various cultures and religions, and has been since practically the dawn of time. Many of the oracles and prophets of ancient civilizations divined the future by entering a state of trance and then becoming possessed by deities. Similarly, many medicine men and priests, belonging to various shamanic traditions, have long utilized spirit possession (as well as spirit control) for healing as well as for prophecy.

The concept of possession by various deities is a vital part of religious worship for many in Africa, the Caribbean, India, the Middle East, and other regions throughout the world. As Rosemary Ellen Guiley puts it, "To be possessed means that a god has found a person worthy to receive the spirit of the god." She further goes on to say that "possession by spirits permeates the daily life" of Hindus in India, with possessed individuals most often being female.

In Voodoo (or *Vodoun*, as it is also known), religious worship involves the possession of devotees in a state of trance by the various deities, which are known as *loas*. Depending on which rites are observed, the *loas* that take possession of the humans who serve them can be benevolent, wise, generous, sexual, vengeful, or cruel. They can also offer protection, punish wrongdoers, divine the future, heal the sick, exorcise evil spirits, give counsel, etc. The worship of the *loas* is an essential part of the Voodoo religion, and it is customary for devotees to propitiate their gods with various kinds of sacrificial offerings.

Possession of a person's mind and body by a Voodoo loa is known as "mounting a horse" and is induced by the sound of frenzied drumming and chanting. During this "sacred interaction" between deity and mortal, devotees lose all consciousness and take on the mannerisms, and sometimes even the physical characteristics, of the particular god or goddess possessing them. Although most possessed devotees return to a normal state when Voodoo ceremonies conclude, such an experience can be terrifying, and even dangerous, for those unable to control the *loa*. Some are taken over by madness, while others are met by death.

131

The Great Serpent known as Dambalah-Wedo heads the Voodoo pantheon. He is said to be the oldest of the ancestors, and the *loa* that brought forth creation. A separate classification of *loas* is the *Guedes*, around which entire Voodoo cults have been known to revolve. The *Guedes*, according to Guiley, "are various spirits of death and dying, debauchery and lewdness, graveyards and grave diggers."

Witches who perform the Neo-Pagan rituals known as *Drawing Down the Moon* and *Drawing Down the Sun* are actually taking part in a form of spirit possession. During the Moon ritual, the spirit of the Goddess is invoked, or drawn down, into the High Priestess, who then speaks while in a state of trance. Similarly, during the Sun ritual, the spirit of the Horned God (the consort of the Goddess) is invoked, or drawn down, into the High Priest. Like his female counterpart, the High Priestess, he too speaks while in a state of trance.

Another type of spirit possession occurs when spiritualist mediums enter a trance during a séance and permit spirits of the dead to temporarily possess them in order to speak through them. There are even some mediums that, while under the influence of a spirit possession, deliver sermons in spiritualist churches. Some also pass along messages from the spirit world to members of the congregation.

Spirit possession is in no way limited strictly to spiritualists and those who follow the Pagan paths. It can be found in both Christian myth and religion as well. According to the Bible, after Christ's crucifixion and resurrection, the Holy Spirit proceeded to take possession of the apostles, enabling them to speak in tongues. (Interestingly, by the Middle Ages, the Church began to associate the once-holy phenomenon of speaking in tongues with demonic possession.)

According to the Hebrew Bible (1 Samuel 16:23), King Saul was repeatedly "tormented by an evil spirit sent by the Lord," which young David was able to drive out by the playing of his harp. "Whenever the spirit from God seized Saul, David would take the harp and play, and Saul would be relieved and feel better, for the evil spirit would leave him."

During worship, many followers of the Pentecostal movement (a Christian tradition dating back to the beginning of the 20th century) believe themselves and others to be possessed by the Holy Spirit. In this state of "ecstatic communion" with God, it is not uncommon for individuals to roll around on the floor, go into seizures, and speak in tongues. To "receive the Spirit," as the Pentecostals commonly refer to this state of possession, is regarded as a blessing.

Spirit Channeling and Possession

Spirit channeling is another term for the invoking, or summoning, of the spirits. An individual who channels a spirit is known as a medium, a trance medium, or a spiritualist medium. To channel a spirit, a medium allows the spirit to use his or her physical body as an instrument through which to speak. However, during a séance or a Ouija board consultation, mediums who do not work with a spirit go-between (known as a "control") oftentimes have little or no control over which spirit or spirits channel through.

There are a number of individuals (many of them Christians) who believe that mediums and others with a high level of spiritual sensitivity are at great risk of being spiritually, emotionally, and even physically possessed by spirits.

133

According to individuals who believe this, there are three basic stages of spirit possession, beginning with what is known as *Partial Influence*. This is when a person feels compelled to spend most of his or her free time communicating with a spirit through some means, usually a Ouija board. Eventually the spirit influences the medium in how to act, whom to communicate with, and so forth. The person's behavior grows noticeably peculiar, and he or she becomes increasingly isolated from family and friends in order to devote more time with the spirit.

The second stage of possession is known as *Partial Possession*, and is the partial control of a person's mind and speech by a spirit. Typically, the dreams and emotions of a person in this state are affected. He or she begins to hear the spirit's voice during waking hours and while sleeping, and begins to fear that the spirit's control over him or her cannot be stopped.

The third, and most serious, stage is *Total Possession*, which requires exorcism. Persons unfortunate enough to reach this point are no longer able to function normally and are often misdiagnosed by doctors as suffering from mental disturbances. They often end up as patients in psychiatric wards or the victims of suicide.

Obsession

The word *obsession* refers to a condition wherein a spirit, usually thought to be evil (or, in some cases, a demon) has a strong influence over a person's psyche. It is defined by the dictionary as, "The act of a demon or evil spirit in besetting a person, or impelling him to action from without." Unlike possession, wherein a spirit or demon takes residence within an individual and gains near full or complete control of the victim's body and psyche, obsession involves external spirits and does not render a person powerless to exercise his or her own will. It can also be accompanied by poltergeist-like activity when the spirit causes certain things to happen around the person it is influencing. Not all cases of obsession lead to full-blown possession. In fact, very few ever do. However, it is said that the state of possession is always preceded by one of obsession.

Much has been written on the subject of spirit obsession, the majority of it being from a negative standpoint and abundant with alarmists' warnings against making contact with the spirit world, especially through séances and Ouija boards, for fear of obsession or even possession. However, not all people (myself included) are of this mind.

The Reverend E.W. Sprague, an ex-missionary of the National Spiritualist Association of the United States of America and a spirit-medium since birth, regarded the notion of spirit obsession as an "erroneous belief" and one that was blight upon the spiritualist movement. Having, himself, been controlled by spirits numerous times while in a state of trance, Sprague regarded his experiences with the dead to be "blessings" and viewed all spirits as teachers whose advice was always uplifting, spiritual, and helpful. He saw the world of spirits as a natural world in which prevailed laws preventing such things as spirit obsession. He did not believe that spirits sought to take permanent or long-term possession of mediums, or possession for the purpose of corrupting one's health, morals, or mind, for sending one to their grave, or for annihilating their soul. He emphatically declared that he was not a believer in obsession and loathed "such a blasphemous doctrine," referring to it in his writings as a "terrible delusion" and "the greatest bugbear to Modern Spiritualism."

In the year 1915, Sprague, writing from his wide experience in occult and spiritual matters, authored a self-published book called *Spirit Obsession: A False Doctrine and a Menace to Modern Spiritualism*. He wrote his highly controversial work in the hope that it would debunk the myths, and alleviate the fears, of spirit possession and allow spiritualism to "be presented to the world in its true light and its beautiful teachings and true philosophy."

To Exorcise a Poltergeist

The following formula for exorcising a poltergeist comes from a 17th-century manual and was reprinted in Wade Baskin's *Dictionary of Satanism*:

"I adjure you, ancient serpent,
by the Judge of the living and the dead,
by the Creator of the universe,
who has power to send you to Gehenna,
that you depart forthwith from this house.
He orders you to do so, cursed devil,
who ordered the winds and the sea and the tempests.
He orders you who ordered you to go back.
Hearken, therefore, Satan, and be afraid,
and withdraw, subdued and prostrate."

Demonic and Diabolical Possession

Demonic possession occurs when a demon takes possession of the body and mind belonging to a living person. In rare cases, dead people and even animals can become possessed. While the phenomenon of demonic possession is universal, it is not as common as non-demonic spirit possession, in which a human spirit or deity dominates a person's body and mind in whole or in part. Even less common is diabolical possession, which is the state of being possessed, not by a mere demon or evil spirit, but by the devil himself, according to Roman Catholic exorcists.

It is believed that when a demon takes possession of a person, it does so gradually and only with the person's consent. In the words of Louis Stewart, author of *Life Forces*, "To the exorcist, this is the crucial fact about possession—it is a choice freely made." After possession has taken place, the victim will begin to display one or more (and eventually all) of the symptoms, which are similar, if not identical, in cases of both demonic and diabolical possession. These include bizarre and unexplainable behavior, violent fits, superhuman strength, the ability to move physical objects through psychokinesis, poltergeist activity, the ability to read the minds of others, speaking backwards and/or in previously unknown languages, and an extreme repugnance toward all sacred texts, symbols, and religious icons associated with the Christian faith. The facial features of a possessed individual are said to often become grotesquely distorted or abnormally smooth, and the body gives off a foul and pungent odor that no amount of bathing can eliminate. He or she will often lapse in and out of a catatonic state and be prone to sudden and unprovoked outbursts of rage and violence.

Interestingly, the victims of diabolical possession have historically always been Christians or others whose belief in the devil (along with diabolical possession) apparently made them psychologically receptive to this type of suggestion. In fact, at no time during my research in this subject was I able to find any documented case histories or other evidence to sufficiently prove otherwise.

Why, then, assuming that the devil did actually exist and that the symptoms of diabolical possession could not always be attributed to mental illness or autosuggestion on the part of the victim, does the devil never seem to take possession of, or appear to atheists and others (Witches and Neo-Pagans) who believe him to be no more than a mythological creature and the figment of some overactive imaginations? Could it be merely that the human mind is sometimes capable of bringing into existence the object of one's fears—whether it is a real or imagined one, as in the case of the devil? I believe that it is. What else could account for the fact that so many, if not all, of the visions seen of Jesus Christ, the Virgin Mary, and other Christian archetypes (including Satan) are experienced by those who had a previous belief in their existence and power?

No records of diabolical possession prior to the advent of Christianity appear to exist. However, by the Middle Ages, nearly every person who suffered from epileptic seizures or exhibited symptoms of mental illness was thought to be possessed by the devil or by one of his minions. Such people were frequently confined to dungeons, tortured, subjected to exorcisms, and even put to death. Fortunately, as medical science progressed and doctors began recognizing and learning how to treat certain mental and physical conditions previously thought to be the signs of the devil at work, the cases of demonic and diabolical possession grew to be fewer and fewer.

The Rituale Romanum

The *Rituale Romanum* (Latin for the "Roman Ritual") is a liturgical book containing all the rites normally administered by a priest, including the only formal rite of exorcism sanctioned by the Roman Catholic Church. In addition to exorcising evil spirits and demons from possessed people, this service manual for priests also contains instructions for the exorcism of homes and other places believed to be infested by the likes of such evil entities.

Written in the year 1614 under Pope Paul V, the *Rituale Romanum* warned priests against performing the rites of exorcism upon individuals in whom no true possession existed. But with the increased advancement of medical science that more accurately diagnosed illnesses of both the body and mind, cases of true possession—demonic as well as spiritual—have become far more difficult to determine. Most of what was previously thought to be demonic possessions are now being diagnosed as schizophrenia, paranoia, multiple personality disorders, sexual malfunction, hysteria, and other neuroses resulting from childhood terrors and obsessions. Since its initial publication in the 17th century, the manual had remained untouched until 1952 when two minor changes to the wording of the exorcism ritual were made.

These revisions changed the wording in a line that read, "symptoms of possession are signs of the presence of a demon," to "symptoms of possession *might be* signs of the presence of a demon." In addition, the original sentence that referred to persons suffering from conditions other than demonic or spiritual possession as "those who suffer from melancholia or any other illness" was changed to "those who suffer from illness, particularly mental illness."

These changes clearly reflect some of the dramatic shifts that have taken place in the Roman Catholic Church, as well as in the thinking of many contemporary Christians who nowadays regard demonic possession and exorcism as little more than superstitious nonsense from the Dark Ages. They also make us wonder, then, how many hundreds, or perhaps thousands, of men, women, and children suffering from mental illnesses were unnecessarily subjected to exorcism rituals in the past.

There are still some priests, in lessening numbers, who continue to believe in the existence of demonic possession and enumerate signs that may indicate its presence. According to these members of the clergy, if an individual demonstrates paranormal abilities, manifests superhuman physical strength, and most importantly, speaks in tongues, then he or she may be a candidate for the rite of exorcism. The church may deem such an individual possessed when the afore-mentioned signs are accompanied by extreme revulsions for sacred texts and objects. A priest trained in the expulsion of demons and evil spirits is then summoned and, only after receiving permission from a bishop, is permitted to perform the centuries-old rite of exorcism.

Exorcists seldom, if ever, work alone. They are normally assisted by a minimum of three other persons. The first of these is generally a younger or less experienced priest who is undergoing training, or has been trained, in the performance of exorcism. His central duty is to maintain the continuance of the exorcism, and to take over the ritual if the exorcist performing the rite should become too ill to continue, or, if his death should occur. The second person that serves as an assistant to the exorcist is, in most cases, a medical physician whose responsibility is to administer any medication or medical treatment to the possessed victim if they should require it. Under no circumstances are exorcists ever allowed to do this. The third person is traditionally a male relative of the possessed person—usually a father, brother, or husband. In some cases he may be a trusted friend of the family. But in either event, it is imperative that he be in excellent health and strong—physically, as well as emotionally and mentally. If the possessed person is of the female gender, many exorcists will arrange to have a woman present during the ritual in order to avoid scandal.

Prior to his performance of the exorcism rite, it is customary for the priest to make a good confession and be absolved of all his sins in the likely case that the evil spirit or demon with which he will engage in battle tries to use them against him during the ritual. He then dons the required attire for exorcist priests (a surplice and a purple stole) and proceeds with the rite.

During the course of an exorcism, certain prescribed prayers such as the *Pater Noster* (the Lord's Prayer), the Litanies of the Saints, and the 54th Psalm are recited over the possessed individual, and often in Latin, as prayers are believed to be more effective when spoken in this ancient tongue. Throughout these recitations the exorcist traditionally makes the sign of the cross, reads scriptures, and sometimes places his hands upon the victim. He also calls upon the evil spirit or demon that has taken possession to reveal its name and nature, to succumb to the Son of God, and to depart from its living human victim and leave him or her in peace. When the evil spirit or demon does finally make its departure, the exorcist prays for Jesus Christ to give his divine help and protection the person, who usually retains no clear memory of his or her demonic possession or of the exorcism. If, on the other hand, the exorcist's ritual is not successful in expelling the evil spirit or demon from the victim, it is then carried out again until the entity takes leave. This can take hours, days, or even longer.

Chapter 6

Spells and Sorcery

Spirit Evocation

Within the perimeters of a clockwise-cast circle, light a white candle to evoke a good spirit. Gaze into the flame of the candle and repeat the following incantation until the spirit appears before you:

By wax and wick,
By flame and smoke,
Spirit of (name) *I now evoke.*
By Hecate's name, materialize!
Reveal thy form before my eyes!

When your business with the evoked spirit is finished, bid it farewell and thrice repeat the following incantation:

Spirit now depart in peace.
Be from this earthly plane released.

Now take your athame and use it to trace the symbol of a banishing pentagram in the air at the east quarter of the circle. (To draw a banishing pentagram, begin at the lower left point of the star (representing the element Earth) and continue in a clockwise manner to the top point (Spirit), to the lower right point (Fire), to the upper left point (Air), across to the upper right point (Water), and back down to the lower left point. After drawing the five-pointed star, immediately draw a clockwise circle around it, starting and ending at the lower left point.) Plunge the blade through the center of the pentagram as you say:

By pentagram, by Hecate's name,
Returneth now to whence you came!

Repeat the banishing pentagram and incantation at the South, West, and North quarters. Uncast the circle in a counterclockwise manner, and then extinguish the candle by pinching out its flame with your fingertips or by using a candlesnuffer.

To Summon a Spirit

Using dragon's blood ink, write upon a piece of dried bark from a willow tree the name of the person whose spirit you wish to summon. Using a mortar and pestle, crush the bark and then mix it with an equal amount of dried and crushed sandalwood.

At the witching hour when the moon is on the wane, place a cauldron at a deserted crossroads and burn within it the bark mixture. Call upon the ancient Greek goddess Hecate to assist you in this rite, and then summon the spirit by thrice reciting the following incantation:

Spirit of the dead,
I call you to me
By the power of goddess Hecate.
Hear me, o spirit,
Awaken from thy rest.
In human form now manifest!

To make a spirit rise from its resting place and speak, necromancers and sorcerers from long ago would steal into a graveyard in the dark of a moonless night and burn a dried and powdered wormwood and sandalwood mixture over the grave of a dead person. Traditionally, the spirit would be made to visibly appear within the confines of a magick circle or triangle ritually drawn upon the ground (from my book, *Herbal Magick.* New Page Books, 2002).

Spell to Enable Contact With a Spirit

On a night when the moon is full, anoint a cone or stick of sandalwood incense with a drop of white willow oil, and then light it with a match. As it burns, concentrate upon the deceased person whose spirit you wish to contact and repeat his or her name over and over in your mind. Continue doing this until the incense has completely burned out, and then proceed to make contact with the spirit by whatever method suits you.

Spirit Ritual

By Jeffrey Parish

With the veil between the worlds thinnest on Sahmain, I use this time to pay respects to ancestors and hopefully commune with the spirit of my departed grandmother, even if only for a moment. My past rituals using the Saints and the Blessed Mother have been quite successful for me in past experiences, so I will share one of them with you now.

You will need the following items:

1. An image or statue of the Virgin Mary or Guadalupe (Guadalupe's Day is the first day of each month, so midnight is her time.).
2. A vase of white roses (Goddess energy and flower of the Divine Mother).
3. Patchouli oil (blessings for the dead).
4. A small dish of calendula flowers (offerings for the dead).
5. Incense (preferably one used for divination) and a censer.
6. Five black candles (five is the number of awareness and psychic endeavors).
7. Pomegranates (wishes and love offering to the Divine Mother).
8. Pictures and/or personal effects of loved one.

Begin set up of your altar early enough to proceed with your ritual at midnight. Choose your altar space so it is to your liking, preferably on a low table so you can sit comfortably, and in an area where you can work with no disturbances. The altar cloth should be a black or dark-colored fabric.

Place the image or statue center to the rear of the altar, the roses to the left with the censer in front of them,

145

and the photo or personal effects on the right with the dish of calendula flowers in front of it. The pomegranates should be laid at the base of the image or statute. Dress the five candles in patchouli oil, and then line them, left to right and evenly spaced, in front of you.

When you are ready, begin in total darkness. Light the censer and allow the smoke to wash over you in its cleansing and protective nature. Anoint your forehead and your heart with the patchouli oil.

Beginning left to right, light the candles one at a time. Try to capture in your mind a fond memory of your loved one for each of the five candles as you light them. After all five candles have been lit, meditate for a moment, picturing each memory clearly in your mind, and then focus on each individual flame as if it were a tiny screen re-playing that particular segment in time. Ask your loved one aloud to remember with you.

When you feel comfortable, say aloud:

> *Our Blessed Lady,*
> *Cleanse my mind*
> *And my heart*
> *Of doubts and fears;*
> *Lift your sacred veil*
> *And allow me to see*
> *If only for a moment;*
> *Guide me, so that*
> *I may communicate*
> *With mine, who now*
> *Reside in your light.*
> *Blessed be.*

Now begin talking. You may talk about anything you like, addressing your loved ones as if they were in the room with you. Tell them how you feel, what has happened since they left, anything! Just talk. Pay close attention to your surroundings. If they are with you, you will know; they give signs. (I always know when the spirit of my Grandma is near; the flames on the candles dance with gaiety and I can smell the scent of Chanel No. 5.)

[Jeffrey Parish is a solitary Witch in San Diego, California. He enjoys many facets of religion, including Catholicism, Voodoo, Santeria, and of course the Craft. This unique blend allows him to explore and expand on his ability to create comforting rituals that all can practice, no matter their beliefs. He is the owner of "The French Country Witch" (formerly "Le Sorciere")—a store that focuses on creating sacred space and surroundings.]

Magickal Oils for Conjuring and Banishing Spirits

To conjure positive spirits to assist you in all of your magickal undertakings, anoint spell candles, incense, charm bags, and other ritual tools with three drops of any of the following occult oils, and then call the spirits into your circle: angel oil, balm of Gilead oil, conjure oil, frankincense and myrrh oil, fruit of the spirits oil, gris-gris oil, heather oil, incense oil, Indian guide oil, kindly spirit oil, lavender oil (to see ghosts), lemon oil, lilac oil, occult ceremony oil (add to bathwater before ritual), spirit oil, spirit guide oil, water of Notre Dame oil, white willow oil, and wormwood oil.

Many Witches, hoodoo practitioners, and other magickal workers traditionally use the following occult oils to banish, as well as to exorcise and protect against, all evil-natured spirits. Many of these oils, such as angelica and unhexing, are effective in the breaking of curses and hexes as well: agrimony oil, angelica oil, banishing oil, birch

147

oil, Ellegua oil, French lilac oil, home protection oil, keep away evil oil, keep away evil spirits oil, mistletoe oil, mugwort oil, mustard oil, orris oil, Solomon's seal oil, unhexing oil, and vervain oil.

Spells to Protect Your Home from Evil Spirits

To prevent evil spirits from gaining entry to your home, hang fennel, garlic, periwinkle, or plantain over all your doors and windows. A horseshoe or a sprig of rue tied with a red ribbon and hung above the front door is believed by many folks to also be effective for this purpose. Planting holly around your home or placing a bay leaf at each of its corners are two other simple ways to keep evil spirits out.

An old method used by Europeans Witches and Christian alike to protect against evil spirits called for Saint John's wort to be gathered on Saint John's Day (June 24th). The herb would then be hung above the doors and windows of houses, as well as barns, stables, and other buildings, to prevent evil spirits from entering and taking up residence.

An ancient magickal method once used by the Assyrians to prevent evil spirits from entering their homes called for five amulets in the shape of dogs to be buried under the front and rear sides of the dwelling. The Assyrians believed that the spirits of the dogs guarded the inhabitants and kept them safe from evil.

Placing the skull of an armadillo above the front door of a house to prevent evil spirits or demons from gaining entry is an old form of Native American "medicine," which is still practiced by some folks in the American Southwest.

If, however, you should feel that one or more evil spirits have already besieged your home, do not despair. There are many proven magickal methods available for making them leave. One is to soak clover in white vinegar for three days in a row and then sprinkle some of the vinegar in each corner of the house while commanding the evil spirits to leave. An infusion of vervain can also be used. Another is to go from room to room throughout the entire house carrying with you a censer filled with dried and smoldering asafetida. This highly aromatic herb is known to sorcerers as the "devil's incense," and is frequently burned during magickal rites to dispel evil. Sprinkling salt, salt water, or holy water (blessed by a priest or priestess) in the corners and centers of each room will also rid your home of evil and unwanted spirits.

Mojo to Keep Evil Spirits at Bay

 To safeguard yourself against evil spirits, some practitioners of the tradition of folk magick known as hoodoo recommend that you wear or carry a white or blue mojo (a hoodoo charm bag) filled with fennel seeds, dried beans, devil pods (also known as "bat nut" and "goat head"), mistletoe, or the roots belonging to any of the following plants: angelica, devil's shoestring, orris, or peony.

To prevent the magickal potency of the mojo from wearing off, anoint the bag every other day with three drops of essential oil of angelica or Saint John's wort—two plants long believed by hoodoo practitioners to effectively ward off evil spirits.

Charm Bag for Protection While Sleeping

For protection against evil spirits while you sleep, fill a red charm bag with cinquefoil (also known as five-finger grass) gathered at sunrise on the day of the Summer Solstice. Hang it above your bed and anoint it every Sunday at sunrise with three drops of any occult oil designed for protection. This amulet is also said to be effective against the sexual night demons known as the succubus and the incubus.

Amulets for Protection Against Evil Spirits

The Pentagram—The symbol of the pentagram (a five-pointed star surrounded by a circle) is one of the most powerful of all magickal and Pagan symbols known to mankind. As an amulet, a silver pentagram offers its wearer protection against all manners of evil, ranging from malevolent spirits to werewolves.

The Cross—For protection against evil spirits or demons, wear or carry a silver cross. The cross is said to be the oldest amuletic symbol, once belonging to the Pagan peoples of Europe and western Asia many centuries prior to the birth of Jesus Christ. It was not until the 4th century that the cross came to be the acknowledged symbol of the Christian religion.

Seal of Solomon—Also known as the "Star of David," this is a powerful symbol used since ancient times by ceremonial magicians to control spirits and to keep the dark forces of evil at bay. In the magickal practices of the early Celts, the symbol of the Seal of Solomon was employed by Druid priests as an amulet to repel evil spirits of the night.

Amber—Regarded as a semi-precious stone, this fossilized resin is said to be one of the most powerful of all natural amulets (made by Mother Nature). One of its many magickal attributes is its ability to protect against evil spirits.

Green Jasper—This gemstone has long been reputed to possess the power to repel ghosts and evil spirits. According to some occultists, wearing a ring, pendant, or earrings in which a stone of green jasper has been set ensures that supernatural apparitions will leave you in peace.

Spirit Stones

In some parts of Africa, where the ancient practice of fetishism continues to be practiced, it is thought that spirits can inhabit certain stones. These "spirit stones," as they are sometimes called, are believed to possess amuletic powers and are faithfully carried by tribesmen for protection against evil. Many African tribal people also believe that spirits can be imprisoned within a stone (as well as within other inanimate objects) by the magickal powers of a fetish priest.

Tree Magick

Trees have long been thought to possess various magickal attributes—among them the ability to ward off evil spirits. For this purpose, the wood, bark, twigs, branches, leaves, and flowers of certain trees have been (and continue to be) fastened on doors, about houses, and in stables. The following types of trees, when made into amulets, are believed  to repel evil spirits: ash, bay, birch, elder, hawthorn, hazel, holly, oak, and rowan (also known as mountain ash).

In centuries past, yew and rowan trees were traditionally planted in many graveyards out of the old belief that they prevented the restless spirits of the dead from wandering about at night.

An old peasant custom, once common in parts of Russia, was to place a wreath of aspen or a cross fashioned from the wood of this tree upon the final resting spots of persons thought to be Witches. They believed that by doing this, they kept the Witches' spirits from rising up from their graves at night and bringing harm to the living.

If you desire not to invite ghosts or spirits into your home, then take care never to burn the wood, or any other part, of the elder tree! To do so, according to superstition, will cause you to be forever haunted by the spirits that once dwelled within the tree. On the other hand, nailing branches of elder above the front door of your house keeps evil spirits from gaining entry, according to an old Scottish belief.

And just as there are certain trees said to hold the power to repel or protect against ghosts and evil spirits, there are also certain trees believed by some people to attract evil spirits like a magnet. The blackthorn and the cherry are two such trees.

Gypsy Spirit Magick

Gypsy Witchcraft and folklore rests primarily upon the belief in certain spirits that dwell within nature—namely aerial spirits, earth spirits, and water spirits. According to author Charles Godfrey Leland in his book, *Gypsy Sorcery and Fortune Telling*, these spirits are "more like divinities, who exert a constant and familiar influence for good or evil on human beings, and who are prayed to or exorcised on all occasions."

The Shamans of old believed that all diseases in both man and beast were brought on by evil spirits that invaded the body and only through magickal means could be made to leave. Abundant traces of this ancient way of thinking can still be found within the practice of Gypsy Witchcraft.

It was once believed that if a sick person ate holy bread (*panem benedictum*) and drank holy water, this would work to drive out the evil disease-causing spirits and the sick person would be made well again. Some Gypsies still carry bread in their pockets to protect themselves against supernatural spirits or ghosts (known as *mulo*), as well as to ward off bad luck.

To keep one's house safeguarded against ghosts, an old book of Gypsy sorcery calls for the skull of a horse to be mounted over the gate of a courtyard or the bones of a fallen animal to be buried under the doorstep. Gypsies have long regarded the skulls and bones of animals as objects possessing great magickal and amuletic power.

To prevent the spirits of the dead from plaguing your dreams, an old Gypsy remedy suggests that you sew a bit of your hair into an old shoe, and then give it away to any beggar you happen to come upon. For protection against evil spirits while sleeping, many a Gypsy Witch (*chovihani*) will recommend that you place a small piece of iron or broom beneath your pillow prior to bedtime.

To Enchant a Necromancer's Candle

Take a black candle that has never been lit, and when the midnight hour is upon you, anoint the wax with three drops of cypress oil. Take the candle in your hands and, as you focus on your intent, repeat the following incantation until you feel the tips of your fingers tingling with magickal energy:

Candle of black sorcery,
Candle of dark power,
Candle I bestir thee
In this witching hour.
Enchanted be by incantation,
Aid me in death's divination.

Spirit Summoning and Banishing Incense

One of the oldest incenses burned by ceremonial magicians to summon spirits is the Incense of Abramelin the Mage, named after a 14th century sorcerer from Germany who believed that to every man was assigned a guardian angel and a wicked demon.

A recipe for this ancient Cabalistic incense can be found in Wade Baskin's *Dictionary of Satanism*, calling for "a mixture of cinnamon, myrrh, olive oil, and galangal." Unfortunately, neither the exact amounts of the required ingredients nor directions on how to make this "fragrant mixture" are given.

After consulting various other sources, I was able to obtain a number of different recipes for Abramelin Incense. The following is one of the recipes:

2 parts myrrh
1 part wood aloes
3 drops of cinnamon oil

Another recipe is as follows:

4 parts frankincense
2 parts storax (also known as liquidamber resin) or benzoin
1 part lignum aloes, wood aloes, cedar, or sandalwood

154

To make either version of Abramelin the Mage Incense, mix together all of the given ingredients and then sprinkle upon a lit charcoal block (the kind sold in occult shops and religious supply stores—not the kind used for barbecue grills).

Hemlock and henbane are two of the ingredients commonly included in many of the spirit-conjuring incense formulas used by ancient sorcerers. These herbs can be very deadly, however, and should be used only with the greatest of caution, or not at all! **They should never, under any circumstances, be taken internally.** If they are to be ritually burned, this should be done out of doors and all precautions should be taken to avoid inhaling the smoke.

A safer incense formula to use for conjuring spirits would be one made from equal parts of anise, cardamom, and coriander. Another effective one can be made from 2 parts sandalwood and 1 part willow bark, and yet another from 3 parts wood aloes, 1 part costus, 1 part crocus, 3 drops of ambergris oil, and 3 drops of musk oil.

To cause spirits to depart, prepare and burn incense made from equal parts calamint, peony, and spearmint. (Some sorcerers also like to add 1/4 part castor beans to this list of ingredients to drive away evil spirits. Be warned, though, that castor beans are poisonous and should be burned out of doors.)

Chapter 7

Herbs Associated With Ghosts

Ghost Flowers

The ghost flower, *Mohavea confertiflora*, is a member of the figwort family. It is an annual and can be found growing wild in the deserts of southeastern California, southern Nevada, and western Arizona. Its name is derived from the ghostly translucency of its cream-colored or yellowish flowers that bloom each year from February through April.

Another ghost flower is the *Monotropa uniflora*, more commonly known as Indian pipe. Its other common names include:

ghost pipe, corpse plant, and fairy smoke. A member of the wintergreen family, this perennial plant is under a lunar rulership and an elemental influence of Water. Its gender is said to be feminine, and its main magickal use is to bring healing after the loss of a loved one. Many folks also use this plant (or infusions made from it) in rituals to honor the dead or to emotionally release a loved one who has crossed over.

One of its other common names—corpse plant—derives from its waxy bluish appearance and its resemblance to the flesh of a corpse. Additionally, the plant turns black when touched by human hands and decomposes rather quickly.

Still another ghost flower is the *Datura*, which is known by various folk names, including: devil's apple, sorcerer's herb, witches' thimble, and *yerba del Diablo* (Spanish for "herb of the devil"). It should be rather apparent from such occult-sounding names that this plant possesses strong ties to the world of sorcery and witchcraft. It is under the rulership of the planet Saturn and the elemental influence of Water. Its gender is said to be feminine.

Despite the fact that Datura is highly hallucinogenic and extremely poisonous, it has been used in spellcraft, shamanic practices, and Pagan religious rites for many centuries. One of its many magickal usages is the breaking of hexes. Some Witches have been known to scatter pieces of the plant around the home to protect the house and its inhabitants from evil spirits and the workings of black magicians. However, this is not recommended if there are children or pets in the house!

157

Other Ghost Plants

Obake anthurium is a beautiful tropical flower that grows wild in the Hawaiian Islands. The first anthurium was brought to Hawaii from Columbia in 1889 by an English missionary named Samuel Damon. The genus name of this plant (Obake) means "ghost" in Japanese.

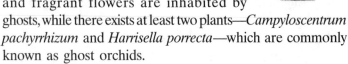

The ghost plumeria derives its name from the old belief that trees bearing white and fragrant flowers are inhabited by ghosts, while there exists at least two plants—*Campyloscentrum pachyrrhizum* and *Harrisella porrecta*—which are commonly known as ghost orchids.

The Spirit Garden

To create a spirit garden to attract wandering spirits, take some dirt from a graveyard when the moon is full and mix it into the soil of your garden area. After doing this, plant any of the following herbs associated with the summoning of spirits: dandelion, pipsissewa, sweet grass, thistle, tobacco, wormwood.

To create a garden devoted to a particular spirit, plant all the flowers and plants that the deceased person was fond of in life, and, if at all possible, place something in the garden that once belonged to him or her. If the person was cremated and you are in possession of the ashes, open the urn and sprinkle a bit of the remains over the garden. Mix it into the soil with a gardening implement or your fingers if you desire. If the person was given a burial, try to obtain a small amount of dirt from the grave and then mix it into the soil of the spirit garden.

Plant the garden on the anniversary of the person's birth or death, or some other day of the year bearing a special meaning to that person (such as a wedding anniversary). It is important that you create it with loving energies and not those of sadness and mourning. As you plant the garden and each time you water it, turn all your thoughts to the person to whom the garden is dedicated. When you feel his or her presence growing stronger around you, you will know that you've connected with their spirit. Should their ghost be observed in or near the garden, let not your heart be struck with fear. Offer up loving emotions and comforting words. Ghosts are almost always in need of love and comfort. (From the book, *Herbal Magick,* New Page Books, 2002.)

Herbs for Conjuring and Banishing Spirits

According to the late Scott Cunningham in *Cunningham's Encyclopedia of Magical Herbs*, Witches and ceremonial magicians have long used the following herbs alike in a variety of ways to conjure forth both good and evil spirits of the dead: althea, anise, balsam tree, bamboo, catnip, dandelion, elder, gardenia, mint, pipsissewa, sandalwood, sweetgrass, thistle, tobacco, willow, and wormwood.

In addition, Cunningham includes the following herbs as some of those used over the centuries by various magickal traditions to banish spirits: agrimony, angelica, arbutus, asafetida, avens, bean, birch, boneset, buckthorn, clove, clover, cumin, devil's bit, dragons blood, elder, fern, fleabane, frankincense, fumitory, garlic, heliotrope, horehound, horseradish, juniper, leek, lilac, mallow, mint, mistletoe, mullein, myrrh, nettle, onion, peach, peony, pepper, pine, rosemary, rue, sage, sandalwood, sloe, snap-dragon, tamarisk, thistle, witch grass, and yarrow.

Saint John's Wort

Saint John's wort, an herb named after Saint John the Baptist, has long been believed to hold protective powers. In Robert Burton's 17th century work, *The Anatomy of Melancholy*, it is said that when St. John's wort is gathered on a Friday and "hung about the neck," it works as a powerful charm to drive away "all phantastical spirits."

Chapter 8

Ghostly Superstitions

Since the dawn of time and in nearly every culture throughout the world, there have existed numerous superstitious beliefs surrounding ghosts and death. Most are a reflection of mankind's natural fear of death and dying, as well as its inherent need to find explanation for the unexplained. Many people regard these superstitions as merely a curiosity belonging to a long ago and unenlightened era. However, old wives' tales die hard, and even in the most technologically advanced societies of the 21st century, superstitions continue to flourish.

In Scotland, it was once believed that a small crucifix made from the wood of a rowan tree and fastened with red thread could offer a person protection against ghosts (as well as sorcery and the Devil) when worn concealed in the lining of their coat.

Long ago, in many parts of Europe, it was common for executed criminals and persons who died by their own hand to be buried at crossroads. This was carried out in the belief that the roads leading in different directions confused the vengeful spirits, thus preventing them from easily finding their way back home and haunting surviving family members.

It is bad luck to dig up a grave. Disturbing a person's remains (whether by grave-robbing or by exhumation for any reason) is said to anger their spirit and cause it to seek revenge against the living.

An old French superstition that survives to this day holds that if a person should unexpectedly receive a visit from the ghost of the last person buried in the year, he or she will meet with death within the coming 12 months.

In times gone by it was customary in various parts of the world for bells to be rung whenever someone in the village died. The ringing of bells not only served to announce the person's passing, but was believed to aid the soul of the departed by keeping evil spirits at bay while it made its way to Heaven.

According to an old superstition, a corpse must be removed feet first from its deathbed (contrary to the usual manner of birth) and coffins feet first from a house. If carried out head first, this supposedly increases the chances of the dead person's ghost remaining in the physical plane to forever haunt the living.

Touching a person's corpse is believed by some people to guard against its ghost from appearing to them in dreams and nightmares. Additionally, touching the hand of a dead person is thought to bring good luck and even cure certain ailments.

In many parts of Scotland, it was once believed that the ghost of the last person buried was given the responsibility to watch over the graveyard until the next burial released it from its lonely vigil.

An article appearing in the *Belfast News Letter* of January 24, 1868 mentioned the old belief that whenever two funeral processions reached a graveyard at the same time, the last corpse in "must watch the other till morning."

If the flame of a candle should suddenly burn blue, this is said to be a sure sign that a ghost is in the room or somewhere in, or close to, the house. According to Francis Grose in the late 18th century work, *A Provincial Glossary* (a collection of local proverbs and popular superstitions), "If, during the time of an apparition, there is a lighted candle in the room, it will burn extremely blue: this is so universally acknowledged that many eminent philosophers have busied themselves in accounting for it, without once doubting the truth of it."

Many superstitious Europeans in the Middle Ages also believed that a blue candle flame was the harbinger of bad luck or, in some instances, death. To counter it, they would extinguish the flame of ill omen by immersing the candle in running water.

An old English superstition holds that all persons having the good fortune to be born in the "chime hours" between midnight on a Friday and cockcrow on a Saturday will be gifted with the natural ability to see ghosts and fairies. Known as "chime children," such individuals are additionally thought to possess wortcunning and healing ways, the power to control all wild and domestic animals, and a natural immunity from Witchcraft and the ill wishes of others. (The "chime hours"—named as such because these are the hours when church bells are rung—are traditionally midnight, three a.m., six a.m., nine a.m., and noon.)

Unlike those born in the "chime hours" (see above), children who come into the world during the hours of Christmas Eve or Christmas Day are said to be unable to see spirits, communicate with the dead, or be haunted by ghosts. This, according to M.A. Denham's *North of England*, is "an incontrovertible fact." Christmas babies are also said to be lucky throughout life and naturally immune from death by drowning or hanging.

To see the ghostly apparitions of those fated to die within the coming year, an old legend says that you must keep a vigil in the church porch between 11 p.m. and one a.m. each year on Saint Mark's Eve (April 24th). On the third year when you do this, you will be able to observe the apparitions passing by into the church.

Cursing the dead is a taboo that exists among many cultures in contemporary times. It can be traced back to the ancient Romans, who fearfully believed that speaking ill of the dead (especially those who had recently succumbed to death) not only disturbed their rest, but also provoked their vengeful ghosts to return to the mortal world and haunt the living.

Neither ghosts nor Witches can harm a first-born child, according to an old superstition. Additionally, a child who is first-born cannot be stolen by, or put under the spell of fairies.

To prevent a dead person's ghost from returning to its former home and haunting the living, an old superstition maintains that the furniture in the bedroom of the deceased must be rearranged while the funeral procession makes its way to the cemetery. This is believed to cause confusion to the returning ghost, prompting it to depart at once and leave the family in peace.

It was customary in former times for mourners to return home from a funeral by a different road than the one used by the hearse to carry the corpse to its final resting place. This supposedly eliminated any possibility of the dead person's ghost from returning home with them.

On the Isle of Man, it was once believed that if the knots of a dead person's burial garments were not undone before the coffin was nailed shut, his or her ghost would restlessly wander the Earth for all of eternity.

When prayers and exorcisms proved ineffective, families haunted by the ghost of a deceased relative would sometimes resort to opening the person's grave, sprinkling holy water upon the corpse, and then undoing the knots in the burial garments.

The curious and widespread custom of covering all the mirrors in the house of a deceased person is centuries old. It is based on the belief that if a person's corpse were reflected in a mirror, their spirit would be unable to rest in peace.

In *The Golden Bough*, James George Frazer offers the following explanation for the old custom of covering up mirrors or turning them to the wall after a death has occurred in the house: "It is feared that the soul, projected out of the person in the shape of his reflection in the mirror, may be carried off by the ghost of the departed, which is commonly supposed to linger about the house till the burial."

According to an old and macabre superstition from England, if an undertaker should accidentally leave a pin in the burial shroud of a corpse, the dead person's ghost will rise up from its grave each night and walk the earth.

There exists an old superstition that a dish of salt and/or earth placed either on the breast of a corpse or underneath its coffin will prevent the dead person's ghost from walking the earth and haunting the living. In some areas of the world (particularly England, Scotland, and Ireland), the old custom of laying a saucer of earth and salt upon a dead man's breast continues to be observed by some undertakers. Some people believe that this ritual also prevents a corpse from swelling and purging. And still others believe that it keeps evil spirits at bay.

Chapter 9

Creatures of
the Night

Vampires

The vampire, whether real or imagined, is a supernatural creature of darkness, and one that has stalked the nightmares, fears, and fantasies of mankind since antiquity. Frightful and evil, yet at the same time strangely romantic and even erotic, vampires remain a constant source of fascination for many in contemporary times. This is undeniably made evident by the strong presence vampires have consistently maintained in novels and films throughout the past century.

Vampires appear in the folklore and legends of many cultures throughout the world from Transylvania (a region whose name evokes images of ancient castles filled with vampires in the minds of many Westerners) to Japan, where tales of supernatural vampire cats and vampire foxes were once told. In Malaysia, the vampire was perceived as a head with trailing entails. In ancient Greece, a strange vampiric creature known as a Lamia was believed to suck the blood of the living. It possessed the upper body of a woman and the lower body of a winged serpent.

However, the Dracula-type of blood-sucking demon that we've come to be familiar with in modern times is largely based on Slavic vampire legends that developed in Eastern Europe during the 9th century. Our contemporary vampires rise up from their graves at night to drink the blood of the living in the same manner as their counterparts in ancient myth. However, the  wearing of capes with tall collars and the ability to shapeshift into bats are not traits originally associated with vampires.

It is believed that vampire bats became linked with vampires in the 16th century when Spanish conquistadors first encountered them in South America and immediately spotted a similarity between the bats' nocturnal feeding habits and those of the legendary vampire. Over the centuries that ensued, the association of bats with vampires spread throughout the world and eventually founds its way into the literary works of 19th century authors James Malcolm Rymer and Bram Stoker, who cemented the linkage of bats and vampires in the minds of the general public.

169

Vampires are described in Louis Stewart's *Life Forces* as "people who by right should be dead, but who remain on earth by sucking the blood of the living. They sleep in coffins during the day. At night, they emerge as tall, gaunt men, flittering bats, or patterns of moonlight." *Webster's New Encyclopedia of Dictionaries* defines a vampire as the "reanimated body of a dead person who cannot rest quietly in their grave, but arises from it at night and sucks the blood of sleepers."

Early Christianity's view on the vampire was that it was the embodiment of evil and sin. Some saw it as God's way of handing out punishment to those who shunned the Christian faith or to those who were perceived by Christians as leading wicked lives. This moralistic Christian view is reflected in the old superstitions warning that a person born out of wedlock, or one who goes to his or her grave before being baptized, will be doomed to forever walk the earth as a vampire. However, just as the vampire was a servant of Satan to the Christian mind, it was, ironically, also beneficial to the Christian religion. According to author Barbara Walker, vampire superstitions were sanctioned by the Church "in order to draw converts through fear."

Back in the days when belief in vampires was widespread throughout Europe, the death of a farmer's cattle or sheep (especially if found drained of blood) was often blamed on the work of vampires (or on Witches).

It was once a Slavic custom to open graves and inspect the corpses for any signs of vampirism. This was carried out three years after the death of a child, five years after the death of a young adult, and seven years after the death of an older person. If an exhumed corpse was found to have one foot in the corner of the coffin, be bloated, have blood in or around its mouth, or show no apparent signs of decomposition (especially if having been buried for a length of time), this was taken to be certain evidence pointing to vampirism. Holes in the earth above a person's grave was also believed to be a sign that the corpse buried below was one of the undead.

In many parts of Europe, it was believed that vampires were most active on St. Andrew's Eve (Nov. 29) and St. George's Eve (April 22)—the latter being a night, like Walpurgis Eve (April 30), when demonic forces, evil ghosts, and monsters of all sorts were supposed to be abroad.

According to an article on Romanian vampires written by Agnes Murgoci and first published in December of 1926 in *Folklore* (Volume 37, Number 4):

> *"In Rosa, it is said that vampires begin to walk on St. Andrew's Eve and separate after St. George's Day, after which they have no power because flowers and the holy sweet basil begin to grow, and this shows the power of God is increasing. In Popeca, vampires are said to be at their worst before Easter. In Mihalcea, they are said to walk only between St. Andrew's Eve and Epiphany (Jan. 6). When the priest sings Kyrie Eleison, all evil spirits vanish until St. Andrew's Eve. In Siret they are said to be free from St. George's Day till St. John's (June 23). The precautions against vampires are taken more especially before St. Andrew's Day (Nov. 30) and St. George's Day (April 23), but also before Easter Sunday and the last day of the year. On St. Andrew's Eve and St. George's Eve, and before Easter and the New Year, windows should be anointed with garlic in the form of a cross, garlic put on the door and everything in the house, and all the cows in the cowshed must be rubbed with garlic. When vampires do enter, they enter by the chimney or by the keyhole, so these orifices call for special attention when garlic is being rubbed in. Even though the window is anointed*

171

with garlic, it is best to keep it shut. Especially on St. Andrew's Eve, all lamps may be put out and everything in the house turned upside down, so that if a vampire does come, it will not be able to ask any of the objects in the house to open the door. It is just as well for people not to sleep at all, but to tell stories right up to cockcrow. If you are telling stories, vampires cannot approach. Women should keep on saying their prayers. They may also beat on the hemp brakes to keep the vampires away. It is unwise to leave hemp brakes or shovels where vampires can get hold of them, for they like to ride on them. Vampires also like to take the tongues of hemp brakes as weapons and fight with them till the sparks fly; hence the tongues should never be left fixed in the hemp brakes. Especially on St. George's Eve, it is a wise precaution to put on your shirt inside out, and to put a knife or scythe under your head when you sleep, turning the cutting edge outwards. It may also be as well to sleep with the feet where the head usually is, so that, if a vampire enters, it cannot find you."

Gypsy Vampire Lore

Greatly feared by the Gypsies are the *mullos*—the angry dead who return as vampires to avenge their deaths. *Mullos* rise from their graves at the midnight hour and sometimes transform themselves into animals, usually a wolf, dog, cat, bird, or a horse. Some Gypsies believe that the mullo remains invisible to all except those who it chooses to be its victims. Female *mullos* are said to possess insatiable sexual appetites and often take human lovers, sometimes even marrying them, but always exhausting them and sending them to their graves. Widows are often targets for male *mullos,* and those who become impregnated by their vampire lovers always bear a short-lived male child known as a *dhampir*. Such an offspring is believed to possess the supernatural ability to detect vampires and is often hired by vampire hunters.

It is a common belief among Gypsies that vampires are unable to cast reflections in mirrors—the reason for this being that they do not possess souls. (Christians once said the same of Witches.) An old belief among Romanian Gypsies was that any person found to be missing a finger or having animal appendages was likely to be a vampire. It was also believed that animals, and even plants, could become vampires and feed off the blood of the living.

To prevent the dead from returning as vampires, Gypsies would drive steel or iron needles into a corpse's heart and placed bits of steel in its mouth, over the eyes, ears and between its fingers prior to its burial. They also believed that placing hawthorn in the corpse's sock or driving a hawthorn stake through its legs was effective in warding off vampirism. Many Gypsies in Romania also believe that certain graveyards are patrolled by supernatural "white spirit wolves" that protect the living by destroying any vampires that might rise up from their graves.

How to Become a Vampire

There are a number of ways by which a person can become a vampire. The first, and probably the most common, is to be bitten by one. Death occurs and then the victim's body returns from the dead as a nocturnal predator requiring the blood of the living to sustain its undead existence. Curses and spells—often attributed to the sorcery of Gypsies—are two other possible causes for vampirism. It is also said that in rare cases an individual can

173

be born a vampire. Many Breton churchmen in the Middle Ages believed that if a pregnant woman exposed her naked body to the light of the moon, she would give birth to a vampire child. In addition, children born with teeth, a caul (a membrane covering the head), or a tail, were at risk of becoming vampires after death. By the same token, persons who had been excommunicated by the church, who died by unnatural means, or who were not given a proper burial, were also candidates for becoming one of the undead.

Superstitious Romanians once believed that the seventh son of a seventh son (and likewise, the seventh daughter of a seventh daughter) was doomed to a vampiric existence after death, as was any child of a woman who was gazed upon by a vampire (or a Witch) while pregnant and did not eat salt (the remedy for such a curse).

During the so-called "burning times" in Europe, many persons who were tried for the then-illegal practice of Witchcraft were accused of vampirism in addition to being in league with the Devil. Such was the case of the Zugarramurdi Witches—a group of 40 persons from Navarre, Spain, who were tried by the Spanish Inquisition in the year 1610.

Methods to Ward Off and Destroy Vampires

Over the centuries, many prayers and spells have been employed for protection against vampires. The wearing of a cross—a symbol believed to be abhorred by vampires and used as a defense against them—is a centuries-old method used by Christians and non-Christians alike. Popular movies and fictionalized accounts of vampires usually depict the cross as an all-powerful amulet operating on its own power. However, actual vampire legend holds that a cross is effective against vampires (as well as other supernatural creatures of evil) *only* if the person using it has true faith in the power of God.

In olden times, it was customary for poppy seeds to be scattered over the grave of a suspected vampire in the belief that it prevented them from preying on the living at night. Juniper branches were, at one time, also placed on suspected graves for the same purpose.

Other preventative measures included piercing a corpse's body with thorns or stakes, placing a crucifix in its

coffin, putting blocks under its chin, or nailing its clothes to the inside of the coffin to keep it from devouring its shroud, and placing a thorny branch of wild rose in the grave.

Silver, a metal ruled by the moon and long believed to possess great magickal and amuletic properties, is said to be effective in warding off vampires (along with werewolves, ghosts, and other supernaturals) when carried or worn in the form of a pentagram. Coffin nails made of silver supposedly prevent vampires and keep the spirits of evildoers contained in their graves. According to folklore, bullets of silver are effective in putting an end to both vampires and werewolves. Some persons also believe that shooting a silver bullet through a ghost is one way of eradicating it.

The brandishing of crosses and garlic has also been long reputed to keep vampires at bay, with both being affixed to windows and doors of houses to prevent the creatures from gaining entry. Holy water scorches their flesh; exposure to sunlight turns their bodies into dust; and a wooden stake driven through the heart guarantees that they will rise up out of their coffins no more. According to some folklorists, a stake is only effective in killing a vampire if it is carved from the wood of a hawthorn, maple, or aspen tree—the latter frequently being the wood of choice for Christians, as it is one type of wood often claimed to have been used for the cross on which their Savior, Jesus Christ, was crucified.

Wooden stakes were not only used to bring death to an existing vampire, they were also used at one time to prevent the recently dead from transforming into blood-drinking creatures of the night. In his book, *Strange Customs*, R. Brasch states, "The bodies of those most likely to transform themselves into a vampire were duly fixed to the bottom of the grave by driving a stake through the heart. This was not merely a physical 'nailing down' of the body, but a magic rite."

An old Bulgarian method of dealing with vampires was to bait a bottle with blood and then place it atop of the grave belonging to the person thought to be a vampire. After luring the restless spirit into the bottle, it would be trapped within by a tight cork and then destroyed by the burning of the bottle.

Montague Summers (1880–1948), a Roman Catholic priest, demonologist, and author of a number of books denouncing Witchcraft as a tool of the Devil, is said to have been an earnest believer in the existence of vampires as actual blood-drinking creatures sent by Satan. According to him, the only effective method to forever immobilize one was to place a consecrated host in its grave. However, such a remedy, in the words of Summers, "was not to be essayed, since it savors of rashness and profanation of God's

Body." (Apparently, Reverend Summers felt that it was better to permit marauding vampires to prey upon the living than to profane Eucharistic bread!)

Other methods used to destroy vampires included cutting off a vampire's head and placing garlic in its mouth, dismembering and burning its body (after which the ashes would be mixed with water blessed by a priest and given to family members as a cure), exorcism, drenching its grave with holy water, and repeating the funeral service.

The Undead

In peace rests not his cursed soul,
But in my bed at night he lies,
Draped in fearful funeral black
Against my pearly nakedness.

My looking glass bears not his image,
Only shadows of the past,
Bathed in rays of silver night,
Which through my windowpane
Come prowling.

Warm and sweet, my scarlet nectar
From his bearded mouth does trickle,
Stains the sheets of ivory lace
With pinwheels red and glistening.

My heart for him alone does beat,
My quivering flesh at his command.
In silent passion, bittersweet,
He tastes my soul,
Then drinks me dry.

[From *Priestess and Pentacle,* by Gerina Dunwich]

Count Dracula

Count Dracula, unquestionably the most famous (or infamous) of all fictional vampires, was a creation of 19th century horror writer, Bram  Stoker, whose classic vampire novel, *Dracula*, was first published in the year 1897. It is said that a sadistic 15th century Romanian prince by the name of Vlad Tepes Dracula (also known as Vlad the Impaler) was the real-life inspiration for Stoker's blood-craving character with black cape and mesmerizing eyes. (The name *Tepes* means "impaler" in the Romanian language, and *Dracula* means "Son of the Dragon.")

Born in Transylvania in November or December of the year 1430 (or 1431, according to some), Vlad the Impaler was the son of Vlad Dracul (Vlad the Dragon), who reigned as Prince of Wallachia—a military kingdom in Southern Romania. Eventually taking his father's place as ruler of Wallachia, he became a member of The Order of the Dragon—a group of Slavic rulers and warlords sworn to uphold the Christian faith by fighting off the advancing Muslim-faithed Turks of the Ottoman Empire.

Vlad acquired his nickname, "The Impaler," from his gruesome habit of impaling his enemies on stakes and, in many cases, cannibalizing their still living bodies. He was also quite fond of putting victims to death by such means as boiling, quartering, nailing, and decapitation. It is said that, during his reign, he killed between 40,000 and 100,000 people—possibly more. He was greatly feared by his serfs, many of whom believed that he possessed the supernatural power to return from the dead and plague them.

It is said that Vlad's days of torture and impalement came to end when he was killed some time in late December of 1476 while engaged in battle against the Turks near Bucharest. His decapitated head was displayed on a pike in the city of Constantinople as evidence of his death, and his headless body was buried at the island monastery of Snagov. Interestingly, excavations made there in the year 1931 were unsuccessful in turning up any sign of Vlad's coffin.

Psychic Vampires

Most rationally minded persons in the 21st century regard vampires as nothing more than harmless (and entertaining) superstition from a bygone era, existing only in the minds of the unenlightened or those prone to fantasy. However, a different type of vampire is known to exist, and the threat of harm that it poses to those with whom it comes into contact is quite real. They do not sleep in coffins by day or feed on the blood of the living by night. Nor are they undead or supernatural. They are, in fact, very much human. Their numbers are great and they can be found both near and far. They have existed since the history of mankind began, and are known as "psychic vampires."

Nearly everyone has encountered at least one psychic vampire in the course of his or her lifetime. Some have been unfortunate enough to encounter many. This type of vampire energizes itself by draining the energies of those around them—sometimes with deliberate intent, but most of the time without even being consciously aware that they are doing it. Where vampires of the blood-lusting variety drain the life force of their victims by sucking their blood, the energy-robbing psychic vampire operates on a more subtle level by destroying the will of his or her unwary victim and leaving them feeling tired and drained for no apparent reason. They receive an energy surge while the victim succumbs to fatigue. Once they find that they are unable to leech any more energy from an individual, they move on to the next unsuspecting victim.

There are many ways by which to spot a psychic vampire. Most are individuals who feel abandoned or rejected, never feel satisfied, often feel fatigued, and are in constant need of reassurance and nurturing. They continually ask questions, seeking ideas and opinions from others, which they soak up. They may also possess an innate desire to control personal and intimate relationships down to the smallest detail, and are usually obsessed with achieving all of their personal desires. Some psychic vampires may suffer from physical ailments, unbalanced emotions, or personality disorders. Many possess violent tempers, which are easily aroused.

In addition to feeling drained of energy, a psychic vampire can cause his or her victim to experience such symptoms as dizziness, muscle tension, headaches, insomnia and other sleep disorders, mood swings, irritability, depression, and even physical illness.

Luckily, dealing with a psychic vampire is relatively simple. The first thing a victim needs to do is to identify the individual depleting his or her energy and then take every step to avoid, or at least limit, contact with them. Using visualization techniques to construct a "wall of protection" or a sphere of white light around one's auric field can be quite beneficial in warding off psychic vampires, as can the wearing of amuletic jewelry—particularly quartz crystals. Never permit psychic vampires to have power over you by allowing yourself to believe that you are powerless against their manipulations or psychic attacks. It is imperative that you firmly believe your will to be greater than theirs.

Spell to Render a Psychic Vampire Powerless

A simple Witch's spell to stop a psychic vampire from draining your energy or psychically attacking you is as follows: Make a poppet (a magickal doll) to represent the person at whom your spell is directed. If you happen to have a photograph of them, cut out their face and paste it over the face of the poppet. If possible, stuff the poppet with some of the person's hair and/or threads from an article of clothing belonging to them.

Charge the poppet by holding it in your hands, focusing your mind on the psychic vampire, and chanting his or her name aloud until you begin to feel a tingling sensation in your hands. Lay the poppet upon your altar between two burning black candles and repeat the following incantation nine times:

Psychic vampire set me free.
No powers have you over me.
By number three times number three,
All harm you've done returns to thee!

After the final incantation has been recited, take a wooden stake and drive it through the "heart" of the poppet to symbolize your triumph over the vampire. As you do this, shout, "So mote it be!"

When the Wolfbane Blooms

"Even a man who is pure in heart and says his prayers by night may become a werewolf when the wolfbane blooms and the autumn moon is bright."

—*An old saying*

Werewolves and vampires share a number of common traits. Both were completely human at one time; both creatures are nocturnal; both possess shapeshifting abilities and an enormous amount of strength; and both prey upon the living. And like their blood-sucking counterparts, werewolves have inspired both terror and fascination in the hearts and minds of mankind since ancient times and have been a popular subject of film and fiction.

"The concept of the werewolf is closely linked to that of the vampire, particularly by the legend claiming that after death, the ghost of a lycanthropist [a werewolf] becomes a vampire."

—*R. Brasch*

The curious belief that a werewolf goes on to become a vampire after death is centuries-old and reflected in the folklore of many European countries, particularly Romania, Germany, Serbia, and Greece.

The *Encyclopedia Britannica* describes a werewolf as "a man who turns into a wolf at night and devours animals, people or corpses, but returns to human form by day. Some werewolves change shape at will; others, in whom the condition is hereditary or acquired by having been bitten by a werewolf, change shape involuntarily, under the influence of a full moon. If he is wounded in wolf form, the wounds will show in his human form and may lead to his detection. Belief in werewolves is found throughout the world. The psychiatric condition in which a person believes he is a wolf is called lycanthropy."

Lycanthropy is a word that derives from the Greek *lykoi* [meaning "wolf"] and *anthropos* [meaning "man"]. It has been used in reference to both those who [by a madness of the mind known as Lycanthropic Disorder] think themselves to be a werewolf and behave in the manner of one, and to persons within whom an actual physical transformation from human form into wolf form [and vice versa] occurs. It is the opinion of many in modern times that the majority, if not all, of the persons believed centuries ago to be werewolves were actually victims of Lycanthropic Disorder.

The werewolf takes its name from the Old English words *wer* [meaning "man"] and *wulf* [meaning "wolf]. The word is said to occur only once in Old English print, circa the year 1000, in the laws of King Canute: "lest the madly ravenous werewolf too savagely tear or devour too much from a godly flock."

Origin of the Werewolf Legend

The legend of the werewolf is believed by many occult historians to have originated in Germany in the 16th century, probably inspired by a rash of brutal cannibalistic murders committed there by a "wolf-shaped man" by the name of Peter Stubbe. It is said that he enjoyed savagely tearing his victims to pieces, drinking their blood, and even dining on their flesh. He confessed, under torture, to being a sorcerer whose shapeshifting powers were derived from a "magical girdle" given to him by the Devil. As punishment for his heinous crimes, his flesh was ripped from his bones with red-hot pincers, his head was chopped off, and his body burned until it was reduced to ashes.

183

In *The Penguin Encyclopedia of Horror and the Supernatural*, author Jack Sullivan states, "the easiest explanation for the werewolf legends is that the wolf was once a creature of terror all over the world, when the earth was covered in forests. At a time when people also feared witches and magicians it was natural that the two terrors would be combined into the legend of the werewolf."

The Church naturally blamed Satan for the plague of werewolves upon the earth, and claimed that the soul of a person afflicted with the curse of a werewolf could not enter Heaven and was doomed to remain earthbound for all of eternity. However, once a werewolf partook of human blood or flesh, his or her soul was eternally damned without the smallest hope of redemption.

Becoming a Werewolf

There are said to be many ways—both voluntary and involuntary—for a man or woman to become a werewolf. An individual bitten or scratched by a werewolf will himself, or herself, become one. The same fate is said to befall those who eat the roasted meat of a wolf or a sheep killed by a wolf, those who drink from a water source from which werewolves have drank, children born on Christmas Eve, and persons targeted to be the recipients of a powerful spell known as the "Lycaeonia Curse." Sometimes such a curse can be handed down from one generation to the next, commonly manifesting itself in the male members of a family. And if a woman becomes impregnated by a werewolf lover, there is a good chance that the child she bears will carry its father's curse.

In some instances the curse can be reversed. Some believe that when a werewolf is killed, its victims (who have become werewolves themselves as the result of being bitten or scratched) become freed from their curse and revert back to normal human beings. This, however, only applies to those who have not yet tasted human blood. For those who have, there is said to be no hope of a cure.

Other ways to end the curse is for the victim of a werewolf to consume wolfbane prior to the first full moon after being bitten. After he or she has experienced the first human-to-wolf transformation, the powers of the plant are rendered ineffective. Another way to bring the curse to an end is by transferring it to another person, but this can only be done during certain rare planetary alignments.

Interestingly, not all persons who become werewolves end up as such because of werewolf attacks or curses. Some become werewolves by their own free will. Eating the brain of a werewolf, wearing or smelling a wolfbane plant, eating human flesh, drinking from the paw print of a wolf, wearing a wolf pelt or a belt fashioned from the skin of an executed criminal, and selling one's soul to the Devil, are all examples of the voluntary methods of self-induced werewolfry.

An old Italian superstition holds that if a man sleeps outdoors on a Friday under the rays of a full moon, he will be magickally transformed into a werewolf. In a similar version of this superstition, it is said that a werewolf will attack him.

Shapeshifting Magick

According to legend, sorcerers and shamans (and, in some instances, Witches) are able to transform themselves into werewolves to attack their enemies and drink their blood. This is often accomplished by donning a special girdle (belt) made of the skin of a wolf, drinking a special potion, reciting certain incantations, sheer willpower, or rubbing a magickal ointment upon the body.

185

Traditionally, ointments for lycanthropic metamorphosis have consisted of such ingredients as the fat of an unbaptized child (some occultists regard this to mean semen), bat's blood, oil, soot, and the following herbs: hemlock, aconite (also known as wolfbane), poplar leaves, cowbane, sweet flag, and deadly nightshade.

A centuries-old Russian incantation for invoking the goddess of the moon and transforming one's self into a gray wolf is as follows:

> "On the sea, on the ocean, on the island, on Bujan, on the empty pasture gleams the moon, on an ashtock lying in a green wood, in a gloomy vale. Toward the stock wandereth a shaggy wolf, horned cattle seeking for his sharp white fangs; but the wolf enters not the forest, but the wolf dives not into the shadowy vale. Moon, moon, gold-horned moon, check the flight of bullets, blunt the hunters' knives, break the shepherds' cudgels, cast wild fear upon all cattle, on men, on all creeping things, that they may not catch the gray wolf, that they may not rend his warm skin! My word is binding, more binding than sleep, more binding that the promise of a hero."

Another ancient spell to become a werewolf instructs the sorcerer to wear a wolf pelt around his waist while he stands in the center of a circle beneath the full moon and repeats the following incantation:

> Hail, hail, hail, great Wolf Spirit, hail
> A boon I ask thee, mighty shade,
> Within this circle I have made.
> Make me a werewolf strong and bold,
> The terror alike of young and old.

Another incantation used by sorcerers in ancient times to magickally induce a werewolf metamorphosis is as follows:

Wolves, vampires, satyrs, ghosts!
Elect of all the devilish hosts!
I pray you send hither,
Send hither, send hither,
The great gray shape that makes men shiver!

Werewolf Lore

Like true wolves, those who are werewolves can live on their own for many years or they can travel in packs with others on whom they have inflicted their curse of lycanthropy.

Vampires are said to be the sworn enemies of werewolves, and are generally more powerful than them. Should a werewolf engage in battle with a vampire, the chances of victory are in the vampire's favor.

If a wound should happen to be inflicted upon an individual while in wolf form, it will appear on the same part of his or her body after the transformation back into human form takes place. At the same time, werewolves are said to be immune from the natural aging process and from nearly every physical disease. This is due to the perpetual regeneration of their physical tissue. However, some sources claim that they are not immortal and, if not killed, will eventually succumb to old age.

According to one legend of European origin, the light blue flowers of the moonflower (a rare plant which blooms from spring through fall, but only under the ghostly light of a full moon) are beneficial for controlling a werewolf's curse. According to another, if a salve made from ten moonflower blossoms is rubbed into the flesh of a dying werewolf, it will remain in whatever shape is held at the moment of death.

187

Recognizing a Werewolf

Some of the typical physical traits of a werewolf are as follows: hairy or rough palms, protruding teeth, slanted eyebrows that meet over the bridge of the nose, and an unusually long third finger on both hands. Certain characteristic markings, such as a birthmark or scar in the shape of a crescent moon, or a five-pointed star on the palm of the hand, are also said to be signs indicating that a person is a werewolf.

Methods to Ward Off Werewolves

Werewolves are said to have a natural aversion to ash trees, rye, and wolfbane—the latter being used as a popular repellant against werewolves in medieval times, despite the legend that the wearing or smelling of the plant induces one to become a werewolf. Garlic and silver pentagrams are also said to be very effective in warding off werewolves.

In France it was once believed that a forked stake surmounted by the head of a horse or an ass served as a powerful safeguard against werewolves, as well as ghosts, Witches, and all evil forces.

"If werewolves are not merely an absurd delusion, then they are evidence of some power of the human mind that we do not at present understand."
—*Jack Sullivan*

Chapter 10

Deities of Death and of the Underworld

Ah Puch is a Mayan god of death and the ruler of Mitnal (said to be the lowest and most horrible of the Nine Hells.) In ancient works of religious art, he is depicted as an owl-headed man and sometimes as a skeleton or hideous bloated corpse.

Aker is an Egyptian god of the earth and of the dead. According to mythology, he watches over the gate through which the pharaoh enters the underworld. He is also the guardian of the place where the eastern and western horizons meet. He is symbolized by a pair of lions facing in opposite directions.

Ament is an Egyptian goddess who, according to mythology, greets the newly dead at the gates of the underworld with water and bread.

Amida is a Japanese god of death, to whom the faithful turn to at the moment of their death. It is said that his realm is filled with ambrosia trees, gentle breezes, and beautiful singing birds.

Andjety is an Egyptian god of the underworld. The rebirth of souls in the afterlife is his responsibility.

Anubis is the Egyptian god of the dead and embalming. He guards cemeteries and burial tombs. According to mythology, it is Anubis' responsibility to weigh the hearts of the dead. The souls belonging to light hearts are taken to the god Osiris, while those whose hearts are heavy are destroyed. In ancient works of religious art, Anubis is depicted as a male figure with the head of a jackal or dog.

Atropos is one of the three Greek goddesses known as the Fates. According to mythology, Clotho spins the thread of life; Lachesis determines how long that life will be; and Atropos brings death by cutting the thread. These three goddesses of fate are said to be older than the gods and have control over the destinies of both mortals and immortals. They were known in ancient Rome as the Parcae.

Azrael, according to the Koran, is the archangel of death who waits over the dying and collects their souls at the moment of death. He is one of the four highest angels at the throne of Allah. It is said that he will be the last to die but will do so at the second trump of the archangel. Azrael is an angel of fiery vengeance—a paradox of angelic devotion and devastating destructiveness.

Balor is a Celtic god of death, and the king who rules over the race of evil giants known as the Formorians.

Baron Cimetiere is a Vodou loa associated with cemeteries.

Baron Samedi is the Vodou loa of death, who controls the passageway between the worlds of the living and the dead. Black is his sacred color, and he is often called upon for information pertaining to the dead.

Chamer is a Mayan god of death, who was principally worshipped in the country of Guatemala. He is said to take the form of a skeleton dressed in white. A scythe with a blade made from a human bone is one of his gruesome attributes.

Charun is a vulture-like Etruscan demon who tortures the souls of the dead in the underworld.

Chertu is the ferryman of the dead and the protector of the pharaoh's tomb, according to Egyptian mythology. He is depicted in ancient works of religious art as a ram or a ram-headed man.

Chontamenti (also spelled **Khentamenti**) is an Egyptian god of the dead and the ruler of the land of the west. He is depicted in ancient works of religious art as a horned dog or as a jackal-headed man.

Chu Jiang is a Chinese god who rules the Second Hell where the souls of dead thieves and murderers are imprisoned.

Cizin is a Mayan god of death whose main function is to burn the souls of the dead. His body is said to be covered with black and yellow spots, and he wears a human bone as an earring. His name means "stench."

Cum Hau is a Mayan god of death, who was worshipped in ancient Mexico.

Emma-o is a Japanese Buddhist god who rules the underworld and judges the souls of the dead. He decides on the punishments of those who commit evil acts based on Buddha's Law.

Ereshkigal is the Sumerian and Akkadian goddess of the dead. Believed to have originally been a sky goddess, she is said to be a deity possessing a dark and violent nature.

Fe'e is a Polynesian god of war and death, who takes the form of a giant octopus. According to mythology, he dwells beneath the ocean with his mighty tentacles reaching to the far corners of the known world like a great compass. His voice was believed to have brought on thunderstorms, the sounds of which were carefully interpreted by the royal diviners of Samoan kings to determine whether or not warring tribes should go forth in battle.

Giltine is the Lithuanian goddess of death and the sister of Laima, the goddess of fate. She is said to appear as a tall and slender woman or Witch in a dress of white (the color associated with death in eastern Europe.) She possesses a poisonous tongue that can bring death to a person merely by licking their face. However, she prefers to strangle or suffocate her victims. According to legend, Giltine frequents graveyards at night, collecting poison from the dead.

Hades is a Greek god of death, who rules the underworld (which also bears his name). He is also the god of riches. Depicted in ancient works of Greek religious art as a dark bearded god carrying a key and a double-pronged harpoon or scepter, he is said to ride in a black chariot pulled by four black horses. His Roman counterpart is the god Dis Pater.

Hel is the Norse goddess of death, who rules the realm of the dead. She is depicted as a frightful hag whose body is half alive and half dead. It is from her name that the word for the Christian abode of the damned was derived.

Heret-Kau is an Egyptian goddess of the underworld. According to mythology, her main function is to guard the souls of the deceased in the afterlife.

Hine-Nui-Te-Po is a Polynesian goddess who rules over death, darkness, and the night. It is said that she is the most evil of all goddesses.

Hunhau is another Mayan god of death, and one of several "lords of death" who rule the underworld. In ancient works of art, he is usually depicted with canine attributes, although he sometimes appears as an owl-headed deity.

Ikal Ahau is another Mayan god of death. It is said that he dwells in the darkness of caves during the daylight hours and roams the earth under the cloak of night in search of human victims upon whose raw flesh he likes to feed. According to an old Mexican legend, Ikal Ahau sometimes takes the form of a vampire bat and inhabits the bell towers of Christian churches.

Isdes is an Egyptian god of death, and one of the minor deities who judge the souls of the dead. He was known from the Middle Kingdom onward, and in later times became syncretized with the canine-headed mortuary god Anubis.

Itonde is an African god of death, who is said to feed on the flesh of rats. He also watches over those who hunt in the jungle forests. According to legend, Itonde uses a magickal bell called the *elefo* to predict where death should strike next.

Ixtab is the Mayan goddess of the noose and the gallows. She is also the patron deity of all persons who meet death by way of suicide. She is depicted in ancient works of religious art as the decomposing body of a woman hanging from a tree by a noose.

Kala is a black-faced Hindu god of death and destruction. In the *Atharvaveda* (an ancient and sacred Vedic text), he is also the personification of time. Consort of the goddess Kali, he wears garlands of human skulls. The putrid stench of decomposing flesh is said to accompany him wherever he goes.

Khentimentiu is an Egyptian god who rules the destiny of the dead. He is closely related to Chontamenti and is often referred to as the "dog of the dead."

Lasa are winged Etruscan goddesses who watch over the graves of the dead. Mirrors and wreaths are their sacred symbols.

Libitina is a goddess of death and funerals, who was worshipped by the ancient Romans and later equated with the goddess Proserpina. She was often invoked during funerary rites and burials, and her name was once a synonym for death. According to mythology, Libitina was the recipient custodian of corpses. Mortuary records, death registers, and all of the necessary implements for funeral services were stored within her temple.

Mania is the Roman goddess of the dead. She is often referred to as the mother of ghosts. She shares her name (which means "insanity") with an ancient Etruscan deity who guards the underworld.

Merau is a Polynesian goddess of the dead and of the netherworld (referred to as Reinga or Milu). According to mythology, she is the rival of the evil goddess Hine-Nui-Te-Po.

Mictlantecutli is an Aztec god of the dead and a ruler of the underworld. In ancient works of religious art he is depicted as a skeleton or a figure wearing a skull. Spiders, bats, and owls are sacred to him.

194

Morrigan (also known as the Morrigan) is the Celtic goddess of war and death. She is a greatly feared shapeshifting deity who often takes the form of a black bird, usually a raven or a crow. It is said that her appearance to a warrior before battle is an omen of his death on the battefield.

Mors is a Roman god of death, depicted in the ancient works of the poet Ovid as a hideous and cadaverous figure wearing a winding sheet (a sheet in which a corpse is wrapped) and holding in one hand an hourglass and in the other a scythe. He is the Roman equivalent of the Greek god Thanatos, and, according to mythology, he is one of the twin sons of Nyx, the goddess of night.

Morta is a Roman goddess of death. Her name comes from the Latin *mortus*, which means "dead." In later times she became one of the Parcae—a trio of goddesses who determined the fates of all mortals. Nona spun the thread of life; Decima assigned it to a person; and Morta brought death to him or her by cutting it.

Mot is the Canaanite and Phoenician god of natural adversity, whose name means "death." He was worshipped in northern Israel, Lebanon, and the coastal regions of Syria from prehistoric times until around 200 B.C. According to legend, he dwells in a pit deep within the earth and his annual death (at the hands of the vengeful goddess Anat, whose twin brother's death he caused) brings drought and scorching heat to the world each year.

Na Ngutu is an African god of the dead, who was worshipped in the western and central regions of the continent. His main function is to guard the souls of warriors killed during battle.

Naenia is a Roman goddess who presides over funerals.

Ndjambi is an African sky god, worshipped by the Herero tribe of Namibia and Botswana. In Michael

Jordan's *Encyclopedia of Gods*, Ndjambi is described as "A beneficial deity who protects and lifts up all who die natural deaths." To speak his name out loud is taboo.

Nehebkau is an Egyptian serpent god who guards the entrance to the underworld.

Nephthys is an Egyptian goddess who meets and teaches the spirits of those who have crossed over into the realm of the dead. She also comforts the members of families who have lost their loved ones.

Nergal is the Mesopotamian god of the underworld, and the consort of the death goddess Ereshkigal. He is said to be an evil deity, whose pleasures are derived by bringing illness, fear, and war to the mortal race.

Ninedinna is a Babylonian goddess who rules over the books of the dead.

Odin is a Nordic and Germanic god of the dead, chief of the Viking Aesir sky gods, and principal god of victory in battle. He dwells within the Hall of Valhalla, ruling over an army of warrior spirits known as the Valkyries. According to Michael Jordan, Odin "is perceived as a shaman, his constant desire the pursuit of occult knowledge through communication with the dead." A shapeshifter who rides upon a winged eight-legged horse, Odin was also the patron god of the battle-frenzied Norse warriors known as Berserkers. Upon death, the bodies of those who were loyal to Odin would be set ablaze on funeral pyres.

Ogiuwu is a West African god of death, who, according to legend, owns the blood of all living things. He dwells in a bloodstained palace in the otherworld, and demands an annual human sacrifice in order to be appeased.

Orcus is another Roman god of death and the underworld. He is also the god of oaths, and is said to bring punishment to those guilty of perjury.

Persephone is a Greek goddess described as the "mistress of the dead and ill-fated consort of Hades." According to mythology, she came to reign as queen of the underworld after being abducted by the god Hades, who seized her one day as she was out gathering flowers with the Oceanides. The goddess Proserpina is her Roman equivalent.

Proserpina is the Roman goddess of death, and equivalent of the Greek goddess Persephone. In a myth nearly identical with that of Persephone's, Proserpina was made queen of the underworld after being abducted by the underworld god Pluto (the Roman equivalent of the Greek god Hades).

Ran is a Norse goddess of storms and the mistress of the dead claimed by the sea. According to mythology, she sometimes causes ships to sink and then collects the drowned sailors in her nets and brings them to her hall.

Rudra is the Hindu god of death, storms, and wind. He is a deity who brings forth destruction and disarray.

Savea Si'uleo is a Polynesian god of the dead. His brother is Salevao, the primordial god of rocks and consort of the earth mother.

Seker is a hawk-headed Egyptian funerary god. He rules over all items used in funeral services, and is the patron deity of those who build tombs for the dead.

Serket is an Egyptian goddess who taught the dead and watched over the canopic jars that hold the bodily organs of mummies. In ancient works of religious art, she is depicted as a woman wearing a scorpion-shaped headdress.

197

Shoki is a Japanese god of the afterlife and exorcism. He is invoked during rituals for driving out demons from possessed individuals.

Supay is an Incan god of death. He is also a ruler of the underworld.

Tate is a Native American (Sioux) creator god. It is said that he appears in the clouds and his voice is the wind. He presides over the changing of the four seasons, and guides the spirits of the dead. Michael Jordan describes him as "the deity with whom the Sioux shamans intercede."

Ta'xet is a god of death among the Haida Indian tribe of Queen Charlotte Island (British Columbia, Canada). According to legend, he is responsible for all who die a violent death.

Tellus is the Roman primordial earth mother (also known as **Terra Mater**), as well as a goddess of the dead. In ancient times, human sacrifices were made in order to gain her favor. It is said that the Romans offered their enemy armies to her and cursed them in her name.

Teoyaomqui is the Aztec god of warriors killed in battle.

Thanatos is a Greek god of death and one of the twin sons of Nyx, the goddess of night. According to mythology, he dwells within a remote cave with his brother Hypnos, the god of sleep. He brings death to mortals, who are then claimed by the underworld.

Tia means "death by violence." He is another god of death among the Haida Indian tribe of Queen Charlotte Island (British Columbia, Canada). It is said that he takes the form of a headless bleeding corpse and possesses the ability to fly through the air. Violent deaths are presaged by the horrible sound of his groaning.

Tokakami is a god of death among the Huichol Indian tribe of Mexico.

Tuchulcha is a demonic Etruscan goddess who guards the underworld. She is depicted as a winged creature with a bird's beak and poisonous snakes growing from her head in place of hair.

Vanth is a winged Etruscan demoness of death who assists the dying. She is said to have eyes on her wings that can see all.

Vichana is an Inca god of death, and the son of Inti.

Wepwawet is another Egyptian god associated with death. According to mythology, he opened the way for the dead into the underworld. In ancient works of religious art he is depicted as a jackal.

Xolotl is an Aztec god of lightning who guides the souls of the dead to the underworld. According to mythology, he is the twin brother of Quetzalcoatl. In ancient works of religious art he is often depicted as a skeleton or a dog-headed man.

Yama is a Hindu (Vedic) god of death. According to mythology, he is the consort of the goddess Dhumorna, and the twin brother of Yami, the goddess of death. His chief function is to pass judgment over the dead, and he is depicted in works of art as a green man in red clothing, seated upon a black bull. It is said that he holds a loop with which he extracts the souls from the bodies of the dead. The black buffalo is his sacred animal, and, like most other deities associated with death and the dead, his sacred color is black.

Yan-lo is a Chinese god of the dead and lord of the Fifth Hell. It is said that he uses memory of things past to punish those doomed to his domain.

Yum Cimil is one of many Mayan gods of death. He is said to take on a skeletal or cadaverous appearance and wears bell-like ornaments in his hair. He was propitiated by the sacrificial drowning of human victims in a sacred pool of water.

Resources

American Ghost Society
515 East Third Street
Alton, Illinois 62002
Phone: (618) 465-1086 or 1-888-GHOSTLY
Website: *www.prairieghosts.com*

American Society for Psychical Research
5 West 73rd Street
New York, New York 10023
Phone: (212) 799-5050 Fax: (212) 496-2497
Website: *www.aspr.com/index.htm*

Association for the Scientific Study of Anomalous Phenomena (ASSAP)
Postbox 327
Bromley, England BR1 1ZE
E-mail: research@assap.org
Website: *www.assap.org*

Austin Ghost Tours
Phone: (512) 695-7297
Website: *www.austinghosttours.com*

Bloody Mary's Tours (New Orleans, Louisiana)
Phone: (504) 486-2080
Website: *www.bloodymarystours.com*

Tim Braun (Spiritual Medium)
P.O. Box 61
South Pasadena, California 91031
Phone: (626) 308-1614
E-mail: tim@timbraun.net
Website: *www.timbraun.com*

Charlotte Ghost Hunters Alliance
P.O. Box 411041
Charlotte, North Carolina 28241
Phone: (704) 661-4932
E-mail: charlotteghosts@yahoo.com
Website: *www.ghosthunters.8m.com*

Chicago Supernatural Tours
Contact: Richard T. Crowe
P.O. Box 557544
Chicago, Illinois 60655
Phone: (708) 499-0300 (daytime)
Website: *www.ghosttours.com*

Crypt Keeper Tours, Inc.
Contact: Corie Craven
P.O. Box 1118
Madison Square Station
New York, New York 10159
Phone: (212) 679-9777 or (888) EXHUMED Fax: (212) 679-9799
E-mail: cryptkeepertours@cryptkeepertours.com
Website: *www.cryptkeepertours.com*

Gerina Dunwich (Medium and Ghost Researcher)
P.O. Box 4263
Chatsworth, California 91313
Fax: (775) 417-0737
E-mail: witchywoman13@paganpoet.com
Website: *www.gerinadunwich.com*

Eureka Springs Ghost Tours
The Crescent Hotel
75 Prospect Avenue, Suite 212
Eureka Springs, Arkansas 72632
Phone: (501) 253-6800
E-mail: ghostmaster@eureka-springs-ghost.com
Website: *www.eureka-springs-ghost.com/tours_offered.htm*

Excursions into the Unknown
Chicago, Illinois
Dale Kaczmarek, Leader
Phone: (708) 425-5163

Ghost Chasers International
Patti Starr, President, Certified Ghost Hunter, Author
1420 Pine Meadow Road
Lexington, Kentucky 40504
Phone: (859) 233-0202
E-mail: hollywood@qx.net
Website: *www.ghostchasersinternational.com*

Ghost Hound

Website: *www.ghosthound.com*
E-mail: contactus@ghosthound.com

Ghost Hunters of Baltimore International

P.O. Box 191
Timonium, Maryland 21094
Phone: (410) 453-2081
E-mail: Ghosthunter@ghostpage.com

GhostNews.com

1732 W. Donner
Fresno, California 93705
Phone: (559) 917-5818 Fax: (559) 297-1062
E-mail: Webmaster@GhostNews.com
Website: *www.ghostnews.com*

Ghost Research Society

Contact: Dale Kaczmarek
P.O. Box 205
Oak Lawn, Illinois 60454-0205
E-mail: Dkaczmarek@ghostresearch.org
Website: *www.ghostresearch.org*

Ghost Tours

P.O. Box 1457,
Sunnybank Hills, Brisbane
Queensland 4109 Australia
Phone: 07 3844 6606
E-mail: enquiries@ghost-tours.com.au
Website: *www.ghost-tours.com.au*

Ghost Tours of Connecticut

157 North Street
Seymour, Connecticut 06483
Phone: (877) GHOST-11
Website: *www.ohwy.com/ct/g/ghotouct.htm*

Ghost Tours of Key West
P.O. Box 4766
Key West, Florida 33040
Phone: (305) 294-9255 Fax: (305) 294-5175
E-mail: keysghoul@aol.com
Website: *hauntedtours.com*

Ghost Tours of Niagara
"A guided candlelit walking tour through the most haunted place in the most haunted town in Canada."
E-mail: ghosttours@hotmail.com
Website: *www.ghrs.org/ghosttours*

Ghost Tracker Investigations
Website: *www.ghosttracker.com/main.html*

Ghost Watch UK
Website: *www.ghostwatchuk.org*

The Ghosts and Hauntings Research Societies (Canada)
Website: *www.ghrs.org*

Ghosts and Hauntings Society
E-mail: ghs@yahoo.com
Website: *www.ghostsandhauntings.org*

Ghosts and Legends of the Queen Mary
The Queen Mary
1126 Queens Highway
Long Beach, California 90802
Phone: (562) 435-3511

Ghosts Of Charleston Walking Tour
Charleston, South Carolina
Phone: (800) 854-1670
E-mail: info@tourcharleston.com
Website: *www.tourcharleston.com*

Haunted Britain and Ireland
E-mail: whiterabbit@afallon.com
Website: *www.afallon.com/pages/whiterabbit1.html*

Haunted Footsteps Ghost Tour and Gift "Boo-tique"
175 Essex Street
Salem, Massachusetts 01970
Phone: (978) 745-0666
E-mail: SalemHFGT@aol.com
Website: *www.hauntedfootstepsghosttour.com*

Haunted Inns and Ghost Tours USA
Website: *www.haunt.f2s.com/tours_usa.htm*

History & Hauntings Book Co. (Ghost tours of Alton, Illinois—Said to be "one of the most haunted small towns in America.")
515 East Third Street
Alton, Illinois 62002
Phone: (618) 465-1086 or (888) 446-7859
Website: *www.prairieghosts.com/tours.html*

Hollywood Hauntings
Website: *gothic.vei.net/hollywood/*

Professor Hans Holzer, Parapsychologist and Ghost Hunter
Fax: (212) 721-6068

IGHS Home Study Course
Certified Ghost Hunter
Certified Paranormal Investigator
Website: *www.ghostweb.com/mainhsc.html*

International Ghost Hunters Society
Dave Oester, DD, PhD
Sharon Gill, PhD
E-mail: MagicDimensions@aol.com
Website: *www.ghostweb.com*

International Society for Paranormal Research
P.O. Box 291159
Los Angeles, California 90027
Phone: (323) 644-8866
E-mail: Ghost@hauntings.com
Website: *www.hauntings.com*

The International Society For Paranormal Research
4712 Admiralty Way (#541)
Marina del Rey, California 90292
Phone: (323) 644-8866
Website: *www.ispr.net/hauntings/index.html*

Invisible Ink (a catalog devoted exclusively to books on ghosts and hauntings)
1811 Stonewood Drive
Dayton, Ohio 45432
Phone: (937) 426-5110 or (800) 31-GHOST
E-mail: InvisibleI@aol.com
Website: *www.invink.com*

John F. Kennedy University Parapsychology Department
12 Altarinda Road
Orinda, California 94563
Phone: (415) 254-0105

London Ghost Walk
Contact: Richard Jones
Phone: 020 8530 8443
E-mail: hauntings@aol.com
Website: *www.london-ghost-walk.co.uk*

Lone Star Spirits
P.O. Box 683101
Houston, Texas 77268
Website: *www.lonestarspirits.org*

Lowcountry Ghost Walk
Charleston, South Carolina
Phone: (800) 729-3420
Website: *www.charlestonwalks.com/ghost.html*

Maines Paranormal Research Association
Phone: (207) 786-0779
E-mail: mpra07@midmaine.com
Website: *www.angelfire.com/me3/MGHA/MGHA.html*

Maryland Ghost and Spirit Association
Website: *www.marylandghosts.com/index.shtml*

Mass. Hysteria Haunted Hearse Tours
P.O. Box 8034
Salem, Massachusetts 01971
Phone: (877) 4-HEARSE
Website: *www.masshysteriatours.com*

Lori McDonald (photographer of anomalous energy)
P.O. Box 20022
Mesa, Arizona 85277
Phone: (480) 699-6597
E-mail: argonaut-greywolf@cox.net
Website: *www.alienufoart.com*

New England Ghost Tours
P.O. Box 812128
Wellesley, Massachusetts 02482
Phone or fax: (781) 235-7149
E-mail: nehaunts@aol.com
Website: *members.aol.com/nehaunts*

New Orleans Ghost Tours
612 Dumaine Street
New Orleans, Louisiana 70116
Phone: (504) 524-0708

E-mail: info@neworleansghosttour.com
Website: *www.neworleansghosttour.com/tours.html*

New York Ghost Chapter
Dr. Frances Bennett, Founder
E-mail: NewYorkGC@aol.com
Website: *www.NewYorkGhostChapter.com*

North East Ohio Ghost Research Team (N.E.O.G.R.T.)
P.O. Box 609
Ashtabula, Ohio 44005
Phone: (440) 228-8939
E-mail: jvarner@ohio-ghost-researchers.com
Website: *www.ohio-ghost-researchers.com/contact.htm*

Office of Paranormal Investigations
P.O. Box 875
Orinda, California 94563
Phone: (415) 553-2588
E-mail: esper@california.com
Website: *www.mindreader.com*

Orlando Ghost Tours
Phone: (407) 423-5600 (9a.m. - 10pm. EST)
E-mail: info@hauntedorlando.com
Website: *www.hauntedorlando.com*

Paranormal Australia: Ghost Tours
Website: *www.paranormalaustralia.com/tours.html*

Paranormal Investigation Team (P.I.T.)
P.O. Box 97
Pembine, Wisconsin 54156
Phone (715) 324-5766
Website: *www.wisconsinghosthunters.homestead.com/intro.html*

Paranormal Investigations

209

Contact: Dave or Leslie Christensen
Phone: (402) 654-2138 (Monday-Friday, 6 p.m. to 10 p.m.)
E-mail: Ghosthunter@midlands.net
Website: *http://www.paranormal-investigation.com*

Paranormal Investigations of South Florida

Contact: Steve Vanik
P.O. Box 814342
Hollywood, Florida 33081
E-mail: flparanormal@aol.com
Website: *www.1freespace.com/ghosthunters/index.htm*

Para-Vision Investigations

Contact: Jeremy Johnson
P.O. Box 1594
Granite City, Illinois 62040
E-mail: help@paranormalworld.com
Website: *www.paranormalworld.com*

Phantom Finders (Paranormal Research & Investigation)

P.O. Box 1054
Kenosha, Wisconsin 53141
Website: *www.phantomfinders.com*

Phantom of Fredericksburg Ghost Tour (Virginia)

Phone: (504) 899-1776 or (888) 214-6384
Philadelphia Ghost Hunters Alliance
E-mail: Rayd8em@aol.com
Website: *members.aol.com/Rayd8em/index.html*

San Gabriel Valley Paranormal Researchers

511 South First Ave. #175
Arcadia, California 91006

Scottish Ghosts and Phantoms

Website: *members.tripod.co.uk/scottishghosts*

Seven Paranormal Research
Contact: Kady Harrington, Director
P.O. Box 1026
Carthage, North Carolina 28327
E-mail: seven@hauntednc.com
Website: *www.hauntednc.com*

Shadow Seekers (a ghost hunting organization based in southeast Pennsylvania)
E-mail: seekers@shadowseekers.com
Website: *www.shadowseekers.com*

The Shadowlands: Ghosts and Hauntings
Website: *theshadowlands.net/ghost/*

Society for Psychical Research
47 Marloes Road
London, England W8 6LA
Phone/Fax: 44(0)20-7937-8984
Website: *moebius.psy.ed.ac.uk/spr.html*

South Jersey Ghost Research (New Jersey)
Contact: Anne Palagruto or Dave Juliano
Phone: (877) 478-3168
E-mail: help@sjgr.org

Spellbound Tours
Contact: Mollie Stewart
PMB #286
203 Washington Street
Salem, Massachusetts 01970
Phone: (978) 745-0138
E-mail: spellboundtours@mindspring.com
Website: *www.spellboundtours.com*

The Spirit Realm
c/o Craig S. Martin
5487 Deschutes Road
Anderson, California 96007
E-mail: thespiritrealm@aol.com
Website: *www.thespiritrealm.com*

Spiritual Frontiers Fellowship
10819 Winner Road
Independence, Missouri 64052
(816) 264-8585

Spiritsearchers (Paranormal investigators located in New Jersey)
E-mail: spiritsearchers@aol.com
Website: *www.spiritsearchers.com*

Spooks: Haunted Texas (Supernatural Phenomenon Organization of Kindred Spirits/Paranormal Research Society of North Texas)
Contact: LaDell Pelzel
E-mail: spooks_tx@hotmail.com *or* spooksprez@yahoo.com
Website: *www.hauntedtexas.com*

St. Augustine Ghost Tours (Florida)
Phone: (800) 527-1177

The Toronto Ghosts and Hauntings Research Society
Website: *www.torontoghosts.org/*

The Transylvanian Society of Dracula
47 Primaverii Boulevard
Bucharest 1, Romania
Phone: 401-6666195 Fax: 401-3123056

Virginia Ghosts and Hauntings Research Society
c/o Bobbie Lescar
4205 Tremont St.

Lynchburg, Virginia 24502
Website: *www.virginiaghosts.com*

Wisconsin Paranormal Research Center
Contact: Christopher D. Claus
P.O. Box 238
Nashotah, Wisconsin 53058
E-mail: wisprc@execpc.com
Website: *www.execpc.com/~wisprc/*

Witchery Tours
537 Castlehill (Jollie's Close),
The Royal Mile, Edinburgh, EH1 2ND
Phone: 44 (0)131 225 6745 Fax: 44 (0)131 220 2086
E-mail: info@witcherytours.com
Website: *www.witcherytours.com*

Yuma Spirit Hunters
12734 El Camino Del Diablo
Yuma, Arizona 85367
Website: *yumaspirithunters.com*

Additional Websites

The Mystical, Magickal World of Gerina Dunwich
www.gerinadunwich.com

Gerina Dunwich's Cauldron
clubs.yahoo.com/clubs/gerinadunwichscauldron

Gerina's Grimoire
iamawitch.com/freepages/grimoire

The Pagan Poets Society
clubs.yahoo.com/clubs/paganpoetssociety

Glossary

Amorphous—Having no definite form or shape. Spirits often appear in mist-like forms.

Apparition—A materialized ghost or spirit. The appearance of a person's phantom, living or dead, seen in a dream or in the waking state as the result of astral projection or clairvoyance.

Apport—A solid object, either animate or inanimate, that manifests during a séance or a haunting by non-physical means. Apports are sometimes made of teeth, hair, feces, or vomit of either an animal or human.

Asport—A solid object that disappears during a séance or a haunting and reappears elsewhere.

Astral Plane—The plane of existence and perception that parallels the dimension of the physical and is the plane that the astral body reaches during astral projection and death.

Astral Projection—Also known as astral travel or out of body experience, this is when the spirit travels outside of the body either to the astral plane or another location on the physical, or earthly, plane; the separation of the consciousness from the physical body resulting in an altered state of consciousness. Astral projections can be achieved by a number of trance-inducing methods or imagination techniques.

Aura—An emanation of energy that surrounds all living things. Many persons possessing psychic abilities are able to see and interpret this energy. Can be viewed as colored lights through the use of Kirlian photography. Many aura-readers believe that a person's physical health is reflected in his or her aura.

Automatic Writing—A method of spirit communication by which a medium enters a trance state and allows a spirit to control his or her hands to write messages. Many parapsychologists believe that this type of phenomena is due to automatism (suspension of the conscious mind in order to release subconscious images).

Banish—To release or drive away a conjured spirit.

Banshee—In old Irish folklore, a female spirit that takes the form of an old woman and presages a death in the family by wailing a mournful tune that sounds like the melancholy moaning of the wind.

As a herald of death, the banshee is usually heard at night under the window of the person doomed to die.

Barghest—In English folklore, a shrieking spirit that assumes the shape of a spectral hound or bear, and whose presence presages a death in the family.

Benign Spirit—A spirit that is not evil or harmful to man. Elementals and spirit guides fall into this category, as do spirits of loved ones that return from the dead to bring us a message or warning.

Bilocation—The uncommon phenomenon of a person or object appearing in two distant places simultaneously. A number of Christian saints and monks were famous for bilocation. It is said that spontaneous and involuntary bilocation sometimes occurs shortly before, or at the moment of, the death of a person whose double is seen.

Channeler—A person with mediumistic abilities who engages in the channeling of spirits, or in other words, allows a person to use his or her vocal chords as an instrument through which it can communicate with the living. One of the most famous channelers in recent times is J.Z. Knight, who claims to channel the spirit of Ramtha, a 35,000-year-old warrior from Atlantis.

Channeling—A term, first used in the 1970s and made popular by the New Age movement of the 1980s, which refers to a spirit's use of a medium's vocal chords while seeming to take possession of his or her body. To channel is to let a spirit speak through you.

Clairaudience—The psychic ability to hear spirit voices or sounds attributed to the dead; an auditory form of extrasensory perception.

Clairsentient—The psychic ability to feel things not normally felt by most people.

Clairvoyance—The extrasensory ability to perceive persons, objects, or events that are out of the range of average human senses.

Clairvoyant—A person gifted with the extrasensory ability to perceive persons, objects, or events that are out of the range of average human senses. Some parapsychologists believe that children are naturally clairvoyant up to the age of 12 years.

Conjuration—The act of evoking spirits by means of formulas or words of power.

Conjurer/Conjuror—A person, male or female, who conjures spirits; a magician.

Conjuring—Any attempt to call upon spirits to help the living, usually for the purpose of personal gain, divination, or to bring harm upon an enemy.

Deep Trance Medium—A psychic who permits a spirit to enter his or her body so that it may communicate with the living. Compare with **Light Trance Medium**.

Deliverance—A Christian ritual designed to rid a person of negative forces or influence. Another word for exorcism.

Dematerialization—A term used by spiritualists and parapsychologists for the sudden disappearance of an item. An asport.

Demon—A low-level and inhuman spirit that interacts in the affairs of the mortal world. It is said there exist numerous varieties of demons. Some are good; some are evil; and some are a combination of both. (The word "demon" means "replete with wisdom" and derives from the Greek, *daimon*, which means "divine power" or "a god.")

Demoniac—A person who is possessed or believed to be possessed by a demon or an evil spirit.

Demonic—Pertaining to demons.

Demonism/ Demonolatry—The worship of demons or evil spirits.

Demonologist—A person who studies demons and their actions.

Demonology—The study of demons and the rituals and folk-legends associated with them.

Demonomancy—The art and practice of divination through the evocation of demons.

Direct Voice—A phenomenon whereby a spirit speaks through a medium in trance during a séance.

Direct Writing—Messages written by spirits without the agency of mediums or other living persons.

Discarnate—A spirit existing without a physical body.

Discernment—To perceive or feel using the mind or senses.

Disembodied—A spirit functioning without a physical body.

Disembodied Voice—A voice heard that comes from no physical body. Also known as EVP (Electronic Voice Phenomena).

Doppelganger—The human double, astral body, or ghost resembling a person who is still alive. The word is German in its origin and means "double walker." Known in Sweden as a *vardoger*.

Double—Another name for a person's astral body or doppelganger.

Ectoplasm—A mysterious substance that emanates from the body or mouth of a spiritualist medium in trance during a séance. Ectoplasm often appears as a white, mist-like substance.

Eidolism—The belief in disembodied spirits, ghosts, or souls.

Eidolon—A phantom, apparition, human double, or astral body.

Elementals—Nature spirits who watch over the four elements. Gnomes are the elemental spirits of the Earth; sylphs are the elemental spirits of the Air; salamanders are the elemental spirits of Fire; and undines or water nymphs are the elemental spirits of Water.

Electromagnetic Field—A field propagated by a combination of electric and magnetic energy that radiates from radio and light waves to gamma and cosmic rays. Most parapsychologists believe that when spirits of the dead manifest, they create an electromagnetic field.

E.M.F. (Electromagnetic Field) Detector—An instrument that measures electromagnetic energy and is frequently used by field researchers of ghosts and hauntings. Also known as a Gauss Meter or magnetometer.

Entity—A disembodied spirit, ghost, or apparition.

E.S.P—Abbreviation for extrasensory perception. A parapsychological term used to denote an awareness of events not presented to the physical or natural senses. Also known as mental telepathy.

Evil Spirits—Spirits whose sole purpose for existing is to hurt or destroy the living. It is widely believed that if a person is evil in life, his or her spirit will remain so after death.

Evocation—The summoning of a spirit, demon, or other non-physical entity to appear, usually within a designated space such as a magick circle or triangle, through the use of spells or words of power. Both demons and angels are evoked in ceremonial magick.

E.V.P.—Abbreviation for electronic voice phenomena. Voices captured on magnetic audiotape when no one is present are believed to be voices from spirits attempting to communicate with the living.

Exorcism—A ritual designed to expel an evil spirit or demon from a possessed person or place. Also known as deliverance.

Exorcist—A person, of either male or female gender, who casts out evil spirits from a possessed person or place, usually by a formal rite of exorcism. In most cases, exorcists are ordained ministers of their particular religion.

Gauss Meter—An instrument commonly used by ghost hunters and parapsychologists that gives a measurement of electromagnetic fields. Also known as an E.M.F. detector or a magnetometer.

Ghost—The spirit or apparition of a dead person that appears to the living or returns to haunt a former habitat; the disembodied spirit of a person who has died. Animals and inanimate objects such as ships and buildings can also be ghosts. Other words for ghost include phantom, shade, specter, and wraith.

Ghost Lights—Strange and unexplained lights that are sometimes observed in haunted houses or, in some cases, graveyards, woods, and marshlands. Ghost lights are frequently captured on photographic film.

Globule—Also known as an orb, a globule is a tiny sphere of electromagnetic energy. When photographed, spirits often appear on film as globules.

Grimoire—A book of spells, rituals, formulas, and incantations designed to evoke spirits, demons, and angels. *The Key of Solomon*, written in medieval times and still in print today, is perhaps the single most famous grimoire used by sorcerers and ceremonial magicians. *Grimoire* is a French word that means "conjuring-book."

Haunted—As a noun, this word is used to indicate a person, place, or inanimate object to which human or inhuman spirits are attached. As an adjective, it refers to a person, place, or object frequently visited by ghosts. From the French word, *hanter*, meaning "to frequent."

Haunting—The unexplainable appearance of an image of a person, animal, or inanimate object on a frequent or regular basis in a particular location. A state of existence under which a human or inhuman spirit has attached itself to a person, place, or inanimate object.

Human Spirit—The spirit of a person who once lived on the physical plane of existence. Human spirits can remain earthbound for various reasons. Compare with **Inhuman Spirit**.

Incubus—A demon, specifically male in characteristics, said to cause nightmares as well as engage in sexual intercourse with mortal women while they sleep.

Infestation—A condition that occurs when an evil spirit inhabits a location. When spirits infests a person or animal, the infestation is called possession.

Inhuman Spirit—The spirit of a creature that has never lived on the physical plane of existence. Inhuman spirits that are benevolent by nature are often classified as angels, while malevolent ones are classified as demons and devils. Also known as a non-human spirit. Compare with **Human Spirit**.

Kirlian Photography—A technique for photographing auras or biofields. Named after the 20th century Russian inventor and electrician, Semyon Kirlian, who founded this process, Kirlian photography continues to evoke controversy.

Levitation—The raising and floating of an object or person by means of supernatural forces, magick, or psychokinetic powers.

Light Trance Medium—A medium through who spirits are able to communicate. In contrast to deep trance mediums, the spirit wishing to communicate through them does not possess light trance mediums.

Malevolent—A type of spirit disposed to evil. A malicious or spiteful spirit. Such an entity often destroys things of financial or sentimental value for the mere sake of hurting someone.

Manifestation—The appearance of, or taking form of, an entity. This word is also used to denote an outbreak of spirit or poltergeist activity.

Materialization—The visible and/or physical formation of a ghost or spirit.

Medium—A gifted person who receives messages, impressions, and other communications from the spirit world. Mental mediums communicate with spirits without necessarily entering a trance state. This is often done by means of automatic writing, direct-voice communication, clairaudience, clairvoyance, or the use of a Ouija board. Physical mediums, on the other hand, generally operate from a trance state, and many produce materializations, apports, rappings, and other paranormal phenomena.

Mediumship—Communication with nonphysical entities, often accompanied by paranormal psychical phenomena. The practice of mediumship, which is both ancient and universal, is divided into two general headings: mental and physical.

Metaphysics—The study of psychical research. Derived from the Latin word, *meta*, which means "beyond," metaphysics literally means that which is beyond the laws of physics.

Necromancer—A person, of either the male or female gender, who practices the necromantic arts. One who raises the dead or communicates with spirits, usually as a means to divine the future.

Necromancy—The art and practice of divining the future by raising corpses or by conjuring the spirits of the dead.

Necromantic rituals sometimes require the use of cremated remains, bones, or other parts of a corpse.

Obsession—The second stage of a haunting where an invading entity begins to dominate the mind of, and exert its power over, its living victim.

Occult—From the Latin *occulere*, meaning, "to hide," a term referring to the body of knowledge that is hidden or secret in the areas of the supernatural, paranormal, or preternatural.

Oppression—The initial stage of a haunting in which the invading entity attempts to gain access to the location or person targeted for victimization.

Orb—A sphere of electromagnetic energy produced by spirits. Also known as a globule.

Ouija Board—A special game board manufactured by the Parker Brothers company and marked with letters of the alphabet, numbers, and the words "yes" and "no." It is used in conjunction with a pointed indicator called a "planchette" as a device for divination and as a means to communicate with the spirits of the dead. Some believe this "communication" is caused by the collective unconscious of the participants. (Automatism.).

Out-Of-Body Experience—Also known as O.B.E., O.O.B.E., astral projection, or remote viewing, this is a state in which a person's spirit leaves the physical body and travels to the astral plane or, in some instances, to other locations on the physical plane.

Outward Manifestation—A term used to describe any event of paranormal activity, such as the sounds of disembodied voices, the movement of objects, vile odors, manipulation with temperatures, and so forth.

Paranormal—A word used to describe occurrences that take place outside the natural order of things. This encompasses ghosts, extrasensory perception, unidentified flying objects, and other things that are difficult to explain by nature but in the realm of the natural.

Parapsychology—A branch of natural science that investigates such things as extrasensory perception (ESP), psychokinesis, and other phenomena not explainable by known scientific laws of nature. Derived from the Latin word *para*, meaning "beyond," parapsychology literally means "beyond" psychology.

Parapsychologist—A person trained in parapsychology.

Phantom—An apparition or specter. Existing only as an energy form.

Phantomania—A term used to describe a type of paralysis that occurs when a person is under attack by either preternatural or supernatural forces. This condition is also known as psychic paralysis.

Planchette—Also known as an indicator or pointer, this is a heart-shaped instrument that, when used with a Ouija board, spells out messages believed to be from the spirit world. It is named after its inventor, the French spiritualist, M. Planchette.

Poltergeist—From the German *polter*, "uproar," and *geist*, "ghost," a word given to the type of phenomenon in which sudden disturbances; such as loud rapping and other sounds; the throwing of objects; the moving of furniture; the raining of stones and other small objects; strange lights; peculiar odors; and physical assaults upon humans and animals; occur. In some cases, poltergeist activity can be attributed to a mischievous or malevolent spirit possessing the ability to move objects by solidifying the ambient air, which results in the movement and teleportation of objects. In other cases, the subconscious psychokinetic powers of a pubescent child or an individual under a great deal of stress may be the cause of the ghostly phenomenon.

Possession—The state of being possessed by a spirit or demon. Different types of possession exist. In spirit possession, a spiritualist medium or channeler will permit a spirit to enter his or her body for the purpose of communication. But in cases of alleged demonic possession, an entity takes control of the host (person) and refuses to leave of its own will. During partial possession, the spirit of the host remains in its physical body; while in more rare (and dangerous) cases of full or "perfect" possession, the spirit is displaced. In such cases, an exorcism ritual is required to drive out the possessing entity.

Provocation—An effort to provoke or command a spirit to reveal itself. See **Religious Provocation**.

Precognition—The paranormal or extrasensory perception of future events, often through dreams or visions; psychic awareness of things yet to happen.

Premonition—A feeling or warning about events before they happen. Premonitions can be either vague or quite specific.

Preternatural—Diverging from, or exceeding the common order of, nature but not outside the natural order as distinguished from the supernatural.

Psychic—A person who possesses the ability to see, hear or feel by use of senses other than the natural senses. A person responsive to psychic forces; one who possesses the gift of paranormal powers. Also a classification of unusual happenings.

Psychic Attack—A physical or mental attack on a human by a spirit, which may be visible or invisible at the time of the attack. There is evidence that certain persons among the living also possess the power to psychically attack others.

Psychic Cold—This is a situation where a person feels unnaturally cold. Two types of psychic cold are known to exist. The first type is caused by a materializing spirit drawing energy from the environment, which results in a lowering of the ambient temperature. The second type is caused by the materializing spirit drawing energy from persons who are nearby. These individuals will experience coldness, even though a thermometer will not register a lowering of the ambient temperature. In some cases, situations of great stress can result in a similar type of cold without a drop in the ambient temperature.

Psychic Imprint—An energy field that takes on the appearance of a person. This usually occurs because of the residue of severe emotional energy, which is imprinted into the environment as the result of some tragic event. While an individual may be convinced they are seeing a ghost, it is actually a projected image, and not a spirit. Also known as a psychic recording or projection.

Psychic Paralysis—A term used to describe a type of paralysis that occurs when a person is under attack by either preternatural or supernatural forces. This condition is also known as phantomania.

Psychic Photograph—A photograph that captures the image of paranormal phenomena such as psychic fogs, spirit orbs, or ghosts. Many psychic photos show only a mist-like form, while in others, the face or other features of a ghost or spirit are discernable.

Psychic Photographer—A person who takes psychic photos.

Psychic Projection—See **Psychic Imprint.**

Psychic Research—The general study of paranormal phenomena, including (but in no way limited to) extrasensory perception, ghosts and spirits, and haunted houses.

Psychic Sleep—A term used for a deep, trance-like sleep from which a person cannot be aroused. Believed by some to be caused by an inhuman spirit, the psychic sleep state usually occurs when an individual is coming under a psychic attack.

Psychic Wounds—Wounds, such as scratches or bites, inflicted by an angry or malicious spirit. Bruising and burns have also been known to result from a negative encounter.

Psychism—Another word for extrasensory perception (ESP)

Psychokinesis—The production of motion in inanimate objects by use of the human mind, either consciously or unconsciously as in poltergeist-like manifestations. Commonly abbreviated as P.K. and also known as R.S.P.K. (Recurrent Spontaneous Psychokinesis.).

Psychometry—The ability to receive psychic impressions of a person, place, or past event by holding or touching certain objects. This process is often used by psychics who assist in police work to find missing persons.

Psychoplasm—Another word for ectoplasm.

Rapping—A way in which spirits sometimes communicate with the living. Ranging from light knocking sounds to heavy pounding; rapping usually emanates from the walls but often sounds as though it is coming from all around.

Reincarnation—The rebirth of a soul into a new physical body. Reincarnation is an ancient and mystical belief belonging to a number of religions, including Wicca. It is commonly associated with the concept of spiritual evolution.

Religious Provocation—An attempt to provoke or command an evil spirit to reveal itself through invoking the name of God or Jesus Christ. This is said to be extremely dangerous for those without proper training, experience, and, most importantly, faith.

R.S.P.K—Abbreviation for Recurrent Spontaneous Psychokinesis. R.S.P.K is the repeated action of objects moving by means of mental power, and is said to be a cornerstone belief of the practicing parapsychologist.

Séance—A gathering of persons to contact and receive messages from discarnate beings or spirits of the dead. Séances are traditionally held in the dark or by candlelight at a table where all persons attending are seated with hands joined to form a circle. At all séances, at least one medium must be present to serve as a channel for spirit communications.

Sending—In Icelandic folk belief, an evil ghost created by sorcery from a human bone, and used by sorcerers to bring death to enemies. The sending is said to appear as a black, smoky shadow with a white spot in its center. The only way to destroy a sending is to stab its white spot with a steel blade, thus changing it back into a harmless bone.

Sensitive—A person who possesses a high degree of proficiency in extrasensory perception.

Shade—Another name for a ghost or apparition.

Shadow Ghost—A black, mist-like spirit possessing no discernable features. Shadow ghosts are believed to be usually demonic in nature and are sometimes described by witnesses as merely a "black shape."

Solidification of Air—The process by which spirits move physical objects.

Specter—Something that exists only in appearance. Same as phantom.

Spirit—A being that exists without a physical body (discarnate) and is not bound by the restrictions or characteristics of the physical world. Also known as a ghost or an apparition.

Suffumigation—The ritual burning of special herbs or incenses for the purpose of attracting spirits and enabling them to materialize. Suffumigations are also used to clear spirits from a dwelling.

Super-ESP—A hypothesis that attempts to disprove the existence of life after death by explaining how ghost sightings and communications from the dead are merely the results of the telepathic and clairvoyant powers of the living. The term "Super-ESP" was coined in the mid-20th century by a psychical researcher named Hornell Hart. Support for this theory has declined since the 1970s.

Supernatural—As a noun (often preceded by the word "the"), this word refers to events that have no natural explanation. It commonly refers to divine acts, but can additionally include extraordinary acts caused by negative forces. As an adjective, beyond powers or laws of nature.

Succubus—A demon, specifically female in characteristics, said to cause nightmares as well as engage in sexual intercourse with mortal men while they sleep.

Telekinesis—Not to be confused with psychokinesis, telekinesis is the projection of perceived movements into a person's mind. An example would be of an object that appears to be moving. The object is not actually moving but it is projected into the mind, thus leading that person to perceive it as a moving object.

Telepathy—The transfer of thoughts from one person's mind into another. Also known as mental telepathy, mind-to-mind communication, and thought reading.

Teleportation—The ability to transport physical objects or human beings from one place to another by supernatural means.

Vardoger—See Doppelganger.

Bibliography

Baskin, Wade. *Satanism: A Guide to the Awesome Power of Satan.* Secaucus, New Jersey: Citadel Press, 1972.

Brasch, R. *Strange Customs: How Did They Begin?* New York: David McKay Company, Inc., 1976.

Coleman, Martin. *Communing with the Spirits.* York Beach, Maine: Samuel Weiser, Inc., 1998.

Cunningham, Scott. *Cunningham's Encyclopedia of Magical Herbs.* Saint Paul, Minnesota: Llewellyn Publications, 1996.

Dreller, Larry. *Beginner's Guide to Mediumship.* York Beach, Maine: Weiser Books, 2002.

Dunwich, Gerina. *The Concise Lexicon of the Occult*. Secaucus, New Jersey: Citadel Press, 1990.

———. *The Pagan Book of Halloween*. New York: Penguin/Compass, 2000.

Evans, Hilary and Patrick Huyghe. *The Field Guide to Ghosts and Other Apparitions*. New York: Quill (an imprint of HarperCollins), 2000.

Facts and Fallacies. Pleasantville, New York: The Reader's Digest Association, Inc., 1988.

Gonzalez-Wippler, Migene. *The Complete Book of Amulets and Talismans*. St. Paul, Minnesota: Llewellyn Publications, 1991.

Guiley, Rosemary Ellen. *Harper's Encyclopedia of Mystical and Paranormal Experience*. New York: HarperCollins, 1991.

———. *The Encyclopedia of Witches and Witchcraft*. New York: Facts on File, 1989.

Hill, Douglas and Pat Williams. *The Supernatural*. New York: Hawthorn Books, 1965.

Holzer, Hans. *Real Hauntings: America's True Ghost Stories*. New York: Barnes and Noble Books, Inc., 1995.

Inglis, Brian. *Natural and Supernatural*. Dorset, United Kingdom: Prism Press, 1992.

Leek, Sybil. *Driving Out the Devils*. New York: G.P. Putnam's Sons, 1975.

Leland, Charles Godfrey. *Gypsy Sorcery and Fortune Telling*. New Hyde Park, New York: University Books, 1964 (second printing).

Linn, Denise. *Sacred Space: Clearing and Enhancing the Energy of Your Home*. New York: Ballantine Books, 1995.

May, Antoinette. *Haunted Houses of California*. San Carlos, California: Wide World Publishing/Tetra, 1993.

Myers, Arthur. *The Ghostly Register*. Chicago: Contemporary Books, Inc., 1986.

Netzley, Patricia D. *Haunted Houses*. San Diego: Lucent Books, Inc., 2000.

Opie, Iona and Moira Tatem. *A Dictionary of Superstitions*. New York: Oxford University Press, 1989.

Pickering, David. *Dictionary of Superstitions*. London: Cassell, 1995.

Smith, Susy. *A Supernatural Primer for the Millions*. New York: Bell Publishing Company, 1966.

Solomon, Maria. *Helping Yourself With Magickal Oils A-Z*. Plainview, New York: Original Publications, 1997.

Sprague, E.W. *Spirit Obsession: A False Doctrine and a Menace to Modern Spiritualism*. Kila, Montana: Kessinger Publishing Company, 1998.

Stewart, Louis. *Life Forces: A Contemporary Guide to the Cult and Occult*. New York: Andrews and McMeel, Inc., 1980.

Sullivan, Jack, editor. *The Penguin Encyclopedia of Horror and the Supernatural*. New York: Viking Penguin, 1986.

Williams, Dr. William F., general editor. *Encyclopedia of Pseudoscience*. New York: Facts on File, 2000.

Wilson, Colin. *Poltergeist: A Study in Destructive Haunting*. St. Paul, Minnesota: Llewellyn Publications, 1993.

Woog, Adam. *Poltergeists*. San Diego: Greenhaven Press, Inc., 1995.

Index

Recognizing a, 188

Werewolves, Methods to Ward Off, 188

Wolfbane Blooms, When the, 182-183

Wooden stakes, 176

X

Xolotl, 199

Y

Yama, 199

Yan-lo, 200

Yum Cimil, 200